SLEEPING GIANT AWAKES

THE STORY OF PORTSMOUTH'S RISE TO THE PREMIERSHIP

by Pat Symes

WITH PHOTOGRAPHY BY MIKE WALKER

The Parrs Wood Press
MANCHESTER

First Published 2003

THE PARRS WOOD PRESS
St Wilfrid's Enterprise Centre
Royce Road, Manchester, M15 5BJ
www.parrswoodpress.com

© **Pat Symes & Mike Walker 2003**

FRONT COVER DESIGN BY Nick Rowley

ISBN: 1 903158 41 9

Printed and bound in Italy

CONTENTS

ACKNOWLEDGEMENTS

When football managers receive their Manager of the Month awards they always credit the team effort when they would prefer to be saying: "If it was not for me, this clueless mob would be bottom of the third division." This book is a team effort in the proper sense. Without Jim Baldwin's facts, figures and explanatory notes, it would never have been written on time and perhaps at all. Any wrong statistics are therefore his fault. Peter Simm and, in Manchester, Rob Dean checked every word with great care and diligence. They must take the blame for any spelling or grammar mistakes. Mike Walker and Mick Young provided the sparkling pictures to record a wonderful season. Wrong captions and picture identification must of course rest with them. Andy Searle of The Parrs Wood Press was the entrepreneurial drive behind the project, nurturing it from pre-Christmas bright idea to the book it is today. As the publisher, any reader-dissatisfaction should be directed at him. Alex Crook wrote the profiles with his usual enthusiasm but there is only one culprit for any errors there. Yes, it has been a team effort and I am happy to accept any praise on their behalf.

Pat Symes
Southsea
May, 2003

PREFACE

APRIL 27th, 2003

FRATTON PARK HAS SEEN many great days in its 105-year history but few would match over the last half a century the fantastic night of April 27th, 2003 when Paul Merson held aloft the first division championship, his blue-shirted arm the symbol of an almighty struggle for supremacy, a battle won and a famous victory achieved. More than 19,400 people roared their appreciation and high in the stands Milan Mandaric wiped away a tear or two. For Mandaric, this was what it was all about: the adulation, the glory, the triumph over adversity. How those happy fans sang... "Toppa the league, Harry and Jim," was a much-repeated favourite but there were others. Queen's old anthem "We are the champions" resounded across the night sky along with "Bye, bye, to

The Fratton End in glorious technicolor.

Celebrations in full swing.

ruled the first division, this was just about the best day of their lives, the day when hopes and prayers were fulfilled and answered. Early leavers rang out a cacophony of noise on their car horns as they spread into the celebrating city and beyond, on to the motorway and out into the suburbs. The whole place was in uproar. Portsmouth versus Rotherham. Who would have thought when that fixture was announced way back in July that the first division championship would have depended on it? Who would have imagined it would have meant so much to Pompey and their now-celebrating supporters?

From the moment nearest rivals Leicester, the only team who could have deprived Pompey of their prize, managed only an early-afternoon draw at home to Norwich, the whole of Portsmouth was a hive of expectation. Leicester's failure to win left Pompey needing to beat mid-table Rotherham to clinch the title. The championship trophy was already secreted somewhere in the city overnight, heightening the tension and increasing the desperation. Surely not even Pompey could

the Nationwide", a variation on a Pet Shop Boys theme, while "Scummers, here we come" pointed to a renewal of local conflicts next season.

What a night, what a season. Blue wigs abounded, blue and white painted faces were everywhere so that for once superfan John Westwood, bugle at the ready, did not seem overdressed. For the likes of Westwood, born long after the days when Pompey blow it now. And they did not. It was not a classic, it was not pretty and Rotherham made it hard. Pompey won 3-2 but the result was simply more important than the performance and when the final whistle sounded, the ancient naval city of Portsmouth took off in a whirl of blue and white and in a blaze of noise.

Fans poured on to the pitch only to be ushered back on to the terracing again by over-worked, beaming stewards so that the presentations could take place. Linvoy Primus had already been acclaimed for his displays with his Player of the Year award. Massive cheers greeted the hugely popular defender who had scooped up monthly awards with astonishing regularity. Later, after a draining and nervous last home match, from the dressing room emerged the players, two-by-two, like some

Harry Redknapp clasps the championship trophy.

SLEEPING GIANT AWAKES

The team is engulfed in a shower of champagne.

latter-day Noah's Ark. The cheers for each couple never abated but noticeably grew as Jim Smith and Kevin Bond were announced as the penultimate pair. But even that was nothing compared with the noise which heralded the arrival on the pitch of Harry Redknapp and Paul Merson, the two men at the hub of a momentous season. It could have been heard six miles away across the sea on the Isle of Wight. It was Merson, the self-styled Aston Villa reject, who stepped forward to receive the trophy from sponsors Nationwide and the decibel level rose again.

"CHAMPIONS, CHAMPIONS" they shouted in delighted unison. Yes, Pompey were heading for the Premiership; promoted with four matches to go and champions with just an irrelevant trip to Bradford to be negotiated. Above it all, happy to let the manager and his players enjoy their moment, stood the upright figure of 64-year old Mandaric, a Serbian-born naturalised American with whom the real glory lay. "Milan, Milan, give us a wave," the fans chanted. They had remembered his part in this unforgettable occasion and the sacrifices he had made to get the club on its feet again after decades of paralysed underachievement. Football's sleeping giant was awake at last and Mandaric was entitled to his share of the rapturous applause and adulation. Alongside him sat guest of

Milan Mandaric, the happiest man in Portsmouth.

honour George Best, a long-term friend, fighting a battle of his own to regain his fitness after a liver transplant. How he enjoyed the night, reliving, just for a fleeting moment or two, the great moments he enjoyed at the peak of his fame at Manchester United. But Mandaric could be forgiven his pride and his tears. This, above all, was his night, the trophy was rightfully his.

Portsmouth is a tight-knit city with a high-density population built initially around the naval dockyard from where Horatio Nelson set sail in HMS Victory and from where battle fleets have sailed for centuries. Football has always been part of the lifeblood so that in the club's heyday, either side of World War II, attendances at Fratton Park were comparable with any of those at other major clubs. But as the navy declined in size and importance, so too did the football club. Bad decisions were made, wrong turnings were taken and before long proud Pompey were a footballing dinosaur languishing in the lower divisions, seemingly destined never to rejoin the likes of once-deadly rivals

Arsenal and Manchester United. There was one glimmer of hope in 1987 when the irrepressible Alan Ball took Pompey into the then first division, but the window of opportunity was slammed shut again 12 months later almost before it had properly opened.

Sixteen years later a unique mixture of Milan Mandaric, Harry Redknapp and sidekick Jim Smith were setting sail for the Premiership, the good ship HMS Pompey afloat once more, all guns blazing. Mandaric, the Serbian creator, Redknapp, the crafty embodiment of London's East End, and veteran Smith, a chunk of Sheffield steel with a penchant for the best red wines. Not one of them had the salt of the Solent running through their veins but all of them had contributed in their distinctive ways to restoring pride and self-belief to a club down on its luck for years and lacking purpose and aspiration. There is still much to be done before Pompey can look the major powers in the eye as true equals but that is the future. The present belonged to the disparate squad gathered together from all kinds of footballing nooks and crannies by Redknapp and Smith, and to Mandaric, the man who financed a collective dream.

When Mandaric was a young man in communist Yugoslavia, attempting to make his way in a regime suspicious of entrepreneurs such as himself, football was his great love. Later in California he made a multi-million dollar fortune in the early days of computing - spotting their potential ahead of others - and from the Stock Exchange but found little real outlet for his love of the game. For a time in the 70s he financed San Jose Earthquakes in the later-aborted American Soccer League, an elephant's graveyard of ageing footballers from across the globe, and which was where he first met Redknapp and Best. When that collapsed, he was obliged to return to Europe to become owner of Nice and Standard Liege without ever finding the passion among French and Belgian crowds that he himself had felt for the sport. There was talk of him buying into Sunderland because he saw in England the one country where football was a quasi-religion, where the game was taken seriously by millions of people in the way he also took it seriously.

It is former Pompey director David Deacon who is credited with first interesting Mandaric in taking over Pompey - then in administration - in 1999 and at a time when absentee owner Martin Gregory was desperate to offload an unwanted and money-leaking legacy from his father, Jim. The club was at a low ebb when Mandaric was tempted enough to spend around £3m on acquiring control. But what had he got for his money? A decaying ground, a team going nowhere and only unwavering and loyal support around which to rebuild an entire edifice. Mandaric set about his task immediately, taking on and dispensing with four managers in ruthless succession. It was only at the end of March 2002, just 13 months before the championship trophy became Pompey property, that Mandaric turned to Redknapp as a last, desperate attempt to make his investment work. By then

Stone, Merson, Sherwood and Quashie say goodbye to the Nationwide.

he had spent some £20 million in keeping the club alive.

As Gregory had discovered, there was a bottomless hole at Fratton Park and nothing to show for it except heartache and disillusion. Only the fans sustained him through those dark days of his first three years as chairman of a club no one else seemed to want. It was then that Redknapp weaved his magic, not sure in his own mind that he had made the right decision to become a manager again, but convinced that if he did not take the job then Mandaric would return to California and Pompey would remain a sleeping giant forever. The rest is a history related in detail throughout these pages. It is a history of prestige restored and power regained.

We must remember also the part played by Fred Dinenage, the easy-going television presenter and the one true Pompey supporter on the board of directors hooked, as he was, while on holiday on the south coast from his Birmingham home. Always self-deprecating, always smiling, Dinenage kept Mandaric on an even keel, raising his spirits when they were at their

Director Fred Dinenage - he knew how!

lowest and keeping the chairman fixed on his true purpose, namely to get the club into the Premiership. Dinenage told the tale of how he had been banned from sitting next to the chairman in the directors' box because in his anxiety to 'shoot into the net' he was ramming his foot into Mandaric's shins. Facing the other way he did the same to chief executive Peter Storrie. In his television-reporting guise, Dinenage had been thrown into the bath at

Bournemouth in 1982 after they had been promoted. His new suit was drenched by champagne after promotion had been achieved in the win over Burnley earlier in April, so Fred kept out of the firing line thereafter, but his influence overall on the club and the participants was not to be underestimated.

The win over Rotherham brought back memories of the first fixture at Millmoor between the clubs which also ended 3-2 in Pompey's favour. He recalled: "I thought I'd go and congratulate the players. However, as I was walking into the dressing room Harry was berating the players for sloppy defending in the second half. As I walked in, Harry turned to me and said quite sternly: 'Yes, Fred. Did you want to say something?' 'Well,' I stammered, 'I just wanted to say well done to the team.' At this point some of the players started to laugh. Harry turned on them and shouted: 'Okay, who would you rather believe... me or Fred Dinenage?' Paul Merson put his hand in the air. 'Actually boss,' he said, 'we'd rather believe Fred.'"

Storrie, too, a former West Ham chief executive, brought order and unification to Pompey's off-field activities but there is no getting away from the fact that, without Mandaric's money, Pompey would not have enjoyed a season like 2002-03. Nor would there have been celebrations like those which hit the city over the next two weeks had it not been for Redknapp's expertise in the transfer market. The colossal number of players brought in - and there was not a dud among them - showed that he had used the chairman's cash wisely.

This fan was in no doubt where the future lay.

SLEEPING GIANT AWAKES

The big day for celebrations was Sunday, May 11, two weeks after the Rotherham result but with the season's triumph still very much in the minds of the city's near-200,000 population. There had been a festive air about the place long before the promotion party began in earnest with an open-topped vintage bus ride from the Guildhall Square through the narrow streets. Fans lined the route cheering from every vantage point, including trees and roofs, as Redknapp, Mandaric and the squad made their way to Southsea sea-front, near to where Henry VIII watched his flagship Mary Rose, all hands aboard, sink beneath the waves in mid-Solent in 1545.

More than 20,000 people were estimated to have hugged the pavements as the Pompey bus, the gleaming first division trophy firmly clutched, reached a specially-erected stage near the Royal Naval War Memorial at the end of a 75-minute journey along Winston Churchill Avenue, Middle Street, Eldon Street, Norfolk Street, Elm Grove and down on to the Common. There the party got into full swing, two hours of musical entertainment adding to a magical occasion. It was time to raise a glass or two, to reflect on the fantastic season now safely behind them and to look ahead to major battles still to be fought.

But it was not always like that. There were tears of a different, less happy kind not much more than a year earlier. The change in the club's fortunes is a compelling tale of glory achieved from the ashes of despair, of success wrought unexpectedly from a background of consistent failure. It is a tale we are happy to chronicle and unravel in these pages.

1

RIX DEPARTS

PORTSMOUTH'S GLORIOUS RISE to the Premiership began well before the summer, way back in March in fact when Graham Rix was hanging on by his finger tips as Pompey yet again flirted with relegation. Over recent years Pompey had always done just enough to get away from the dreaded drop, but it was too often achieved only on or near the last day of the season, narrowly evading the clutches of the second division. Certainly it was not the sort of scenario expected by the heavily-investing chairman when he first took over, and as the end of the 2001-02 season approached Pompey fears of relegation had only recently been extinguished. It was a situation which clearly could not continue indefinitely. Mandaric knew it, Redknapp, as director of football, knew it and so too did the luckless Rix.

The former Arsenal and England player had built a formidable reputation as a coach in successful and entertaining Chelsea sides alongside Ruud Gullit and Gianluca Vialli but his allotted lifespan (13 months) at Fratton Park was coming to an end and fans, commentators, staff and Rix himself were all aware of his impending execution. Had Redknapp been so inclined he could even have had the manager's job two months earlier in January when Pompey were so humiliatingly knocked out of the FA Cup at home by third division Leyton Orient, but the timing was not right and Rix survived... just.

**Graham Rix
- running out of time.**

In the dark over Todorov.

The first signs of Rix's imminent demise, and his replacement by Redknapp, came with the signing of Svetoslav Todorov from West Ham on March 19, six days before Redknapp emerged at last from his management exile to take charge of playing affairs. Rix said: "I don't know anything about Todorov. I have never even seen him play." This was a clear indication that the Bulgarian international was a Redknapp man, the deal had been fixed by Redknapp and Rix had been completely bypassed. While Rix expressed his unease, Todorov appeared from the outside to be an unusual first signing by Redknapp. He had fallen by the wayside at West Ham after Redknapp's departure, had failed to do himself justice on the few occasions Glenn Roeder had picked him, and showed all the signs of feeling sorry for himself on the sidelines. There was no obvious West Ham protest when Redknapp persuaded the chairman to pay £750,000 for a player others might have considered temperamental and whose record at West Ham showed just one Premiership goal in 14 matches. How wrong they all were. Todorov, after a slow start at Pompey when opinions were reserved, emerged in 2002-03 as a tremendous signing full of guile, pace, skill and Premiership-quality finishing.

The big day was March 25 when Rix was told by telephone that his services were no longer required and Redknapp, his appetite restored by his sabbatical, assumed command with all his old wit and flair for publicity. The red fox was back and loving every minute of the press conference called at Fratton Park to announce his return to management. The Upton Park saga had hurt him deeply and his famous son Jamie, sensing his father's tiredness and sense of betrayal, even suggested that at 55 he had managed for the last time. But the spell out of the game, his first in 20 years of management, had patently done him good and restored him to good health for the massive task ahead. For Mandaric it was a last desperate gamble after three years and

Todorov
- an inspired early signing.

soccer at Phoenix soon after Redknapp, with a young family in tow, had joined them that persuaded the future Pompey boss to return to England after some eight years in America. Luckily for him there was a coaching vacancy at his old club Bournemouth where Dave Webb was in charge and, when Webb moved on acrimoniously soon afterwards and his replacement Don Megson lasted a matter of months, Redknapp became manager, on his own admission, almost by default. There was a quote from him at the time in 1983 when he said he was interested only in coaching and that there was one certainty about becoming a manager - the sack followed.

So what could Redknapp achieve that in the Mandaric years Alan Ball, Tony Pulis, Steve Claridge and Rix could not? From 1994 until 2001 he had been a Premiership manager at West Ham, taking the Hammers to fifth place and into Europe in the UEFA Cup and the much-derided Intertoto Cup. Derided, that is, until you win it, as West Ham did in 1999. Along the way he forged a reputation for wheeling and dealing in the transfer market, perhaps more frequently than any of his contemporaries, and while some of his deals had not always been successful, many others had proved a canny eye for flair players. Trevor Sinclair, Frederic Kanoute and Paolo Di

some £20 million had been wasted on a succession of managers and their follies and failures. He had known Redknapp from the United States where he was financing San Jose Earthquakes in the failed American Soccer League and where Redknapp was winding down his own playing career at Seattle and, disastrously, at the bankrupt Phoenix. It was the collapse of

Redknapp assumes command.

Canio were three he had brought to West Ham, while talented youngsters Joe Cole, Rio Ferdinand, Jermain Defoe and Michael Carrick were swiftly promoted through the youth system, all of them typical of the sort of players Redknapp revered and encouraged. Redknapp teams at Bournemouth over nine years and West Ham over another seven always played 'football' in the purest sense, never compromising the standards set for him by Ron Greenwood when he was a teenage novice fresh from the East End.

At Bournemouth on a limited budget he had taken the perennially penniless Cherries into what was then the second division in 1987 as champions and had inflicted one of the greatest of post-war FA Cup surprises three years earlier when his team of journeymen had beaten Ron Atkinson's cup holders, Manchester United, 2-0 at Dean Court. It was that result which first brought him to the attention of the footballing world and marked him out as a young man with potential for greater things.

RIX DEPARTS

At West Ham his teams always had a reputation for playing in an entertaining fashion home and away. There were good results and bad but on their day, all departments firing, they could beat any Premiership rival at any time. The FA Cup win at Manchester United in the fourth round in 2001 was an example of the best but the Hammers never shook off the unwanted label of also being something of a soft touch in his time, losing at places like Wrexham and Tranmere when primitive passion got the better of class and superior skill.

So Redknapp, much respected though he deserved to be, did not have much in the way of silverware to commend him to the chairman. His success had come through an accumulation of outstanding individual results and a loveable, rascally image rather than a solid phalanx of table-topping achievement spread over his years in the precarious business of football management. Despite his early fears, he had only ever been fired once - in a messy finale at West Ham in 2001 when his relationship with Hammers chairman Terry Brown had broken down irretrievably. Mandaric had a contrastingly strong faith in his latest manager and made it clear at the press conference that morning in March that should Redknapp fail, as his predecessors had done so spectacularly, he would

depart for his adopted home in Florida a chastened and wiser man, his wealth much reduced by his quest to turn Pompey into a footballing power. It was do or die and as Redknapp said: "Portsmouth might be a sleeping giant but unless someone revives it quickly, it will never wake up." Against this background Redknapp took control of a playing staff numbering some 45 players and with once-proud Portsmouth in a desultory 15th position in the first division. The Premiership was a distant dream, a land inhabited by another footballing species.

Pompey were at least safe from relegation but the transfer deadline was a matter of days away and there was still a handful of fixtures left to be fulfilled before the long summer months could at least give the new boss the chance to start his task of revamping his squad. It was not going to be easy, and Redknapp did not waste a single moment. Having told the press conference he did not think he would indulge in the pre-deadline frenzy of transfer activity because there was no need, the new manager leapt in with both feet almost immediately, brandishing Mandaric's cheque book, as the chairman promised he could.

To the disappointment of all Pompey fans who had come to appreciate his awkward, gangling but surprisingly deft qualities, lanky Peter Crouch was sold to Aston Villa after scoring 18 goals in 37 matches. Rix must take credit for the Crouch signing, a mere £1.25m from Queen's Park Rangers and while Rangers collected a third of the profit, Pompey still made a handsome gain from the deal when he was sold eight months later for an appearance-based £5m. Crouch's subsequent lack of success at Aston Villa was a source of mystery to Pompey fans who were hardly delighted that the new manager, virtually as his first act, had sold the club's best player and not lined up a replacement. Redknapp said Villa's offer was too good to refuse and it was obvious from his tone that it was to be the first of many player moves over the next hectic 13 months. How many not even the most fevered

**Peter Crouch - surprisingly deft qualities
and a big profit.**

Pompey imagination could grasp.

Redknapp's first act was to return to his old club, Bournemouth, to pay £400,000 for their England under-21 international defender Eddie Howe. There was no doubting Howe's quality and Bournemouth had hoped, as relegation neared, to earn more for their best player. As an ex-player and manager at Dean Court, Redknapp was acutely aware that by taking their best defender he was leaving Bournemouth in a vulnerable position and indeed they failed to stay up. Howe had reached the stage of his career where he needed a move. At 24 he had made 200 appearances for Bournemouth but for a player of his ability and ambition the second division, or worse, the third, was no good to him. Redknapp said: "Eddie is a top class lad. I have kept an eye on his career from close quarters. He has a great attitude and he will go on to play 200 games for Portsmouth. He is reliable and steady." Steady Eddie, as they knew him at Bournemouth, sadly got little chance to justify Redknapp's decision to lure him along the south coast. Howe lasted less than one half at Preston in his first match a few days later and barely five minutes of the opening fixture of the next season at home to Nottingham Forest. He limped off with a knee injury and spent the rest of the

'Steady' Eddie Howe - £400,000 from Redknapp's first club Bournemouth but injury meant he has played in only two games.

year, as Pompey stormed forward, trying to find a cure. Even a trip to America for specialist treatment in February could not prevent him missing in effect the whole of 2002-03.

On the same day, Redknapp and chief executive Peter Storrie began the process of unloading those players accumulated by four different managers in three years. Many had been left to rot

Ceri Hughes - eight caps for Wales but persistent knee injuries limited his appearances.

in the reserves, or were simply ignored, as each new boss brought in new ones and discarded those they had inherited. Ceri Hughes was a case in point. Signed by Tony Pulis from Wimbledon for £100,000, he had been a good enough player to earn eight Welsh caps but persistent knee injuries limited him to 34 appearances for Pompey and he did not play at all for Claridge or Rix. Redknapp was quick to allow him to take up the chance of a trial at Cardiff, the club he had supported as a boy.

RIX DEPARTS

But it meant paying him up the remainder of his contract, as Pompey were forced to do time and again over the following months simply to make space. Hughes was swiftly followed by others. Andy Petterson, an Australian goalkeeper signed by Ball, joined West Brom for the remainder of the season.

Petterson made a big impression when he first joined Pompey on loan from Charlton, so big that before his return to Charlton, fans made a special presentation to him. Typical of the way things went at Fratton Park, Pulis dropped him after one match and signed Russell Hoult instead. Hoult and Pulis came and went and Petterson was still languishing in the background when Claridge and Rix followed him out of Fratton Park. This time there was no presentation when he finally moved on.

Departing, too, was Dave Waterman, a tough-tackling and versatile Channel Islander, who never gave less than 100 per cent for Pompey and was well regarded by fans, partly on the basis that he had joined as a 16-year old and had gone on to make 80 appearances. Many were sorry to see him go, but when Oxford United came in, Redknapp let him move on for nothing. A revolution was taking place and in all revolutions there are casualties. No one quite knew what to make of Michael Panopoulos, the Greek-Australian who could never add consistency to his undoubted talent. Alan Ball liked him enough to pay £500,000 but his successors did not share his enthusiasm. End of story. Panopoulos had a short spell on loan at Dunfermline but once Pompey agreed to pay him up,

Andy Petterson - from Down Under and Out.

he was off to Australia, his ability never fully tested.

But the transfer moves in and out were not over by any means. Redknapp wanted to use the last few matches of the season to look at potential newcomers for the following year so he temporarily recruited Scott Wilson, a strong defender from Rangers, and Mark Summerbell, a busy midfield player who had Premiership experience at Middlesbrough without holding down a place. With Pompey fending off late interest from Charlton in Howe, all three were pitched in at Preston for Redknapp's first match in charge. Goalless at half time, Pompey let in two in the second half and as Howe limped off, travelling fans wondered if this really was the start of a brave new chapter in the club's history. Frankly, it did not look like it.

One other issue remained to be resolved. Who was going to be Redknapp's number two? His brother-in-law Frank Lampard had fulfilled that role at West Ham and had gone from Upton Park at the same time as Redknapp. But it was clear, despite visits to Fratton Park, that he was not going to be coming to Pompey. Rumours, and there were always plenty of those, linked Pompey with Steve Cotterill, the bright young manager of Cheltenham. Cotterill had taken Cheltenham into the second division from the depths of

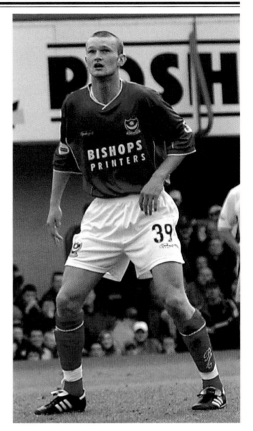

Scott Wilson - strong defender from Rangers.

the Dr Marten's League and had outgrown the homely Gloucestershire club. Other clubs had noticed his astonishing progress and what he had achieved with resources bordering on the non-existent. The rumours were further fuelled by the sight of Cotterill and Redknapp sitting together in the stands at Bournemouth one evening. The fact that both lived in Bournemouth was also a link. Redknapp added to it when he said: "I know Steve and respect what he has done. He is a bright young manager with a big future. Of course I would be interested in having him here." Cheltenham did not see that as a direct approach for their manager but they knew he would not stay and in due course left for Stoke and then, dramatically, for Sunderland as number two to Howard Wilkinson. Graham Rix's deputy, Jim Duffy, had left after the Orient debacle, ultimately for Dundee, enabling Neil McNab to be promoted, but there was no way Redknapp was going to keep McNab at his side for very long, and so it proved. A matter of days, in fact. The search for an assistant manager was to continue later and at this stage of a dying season it was not a priority.

As for Redknapp, the week of indulging himself in the transfer market had revived him, reminding himself of what he did best and providing oxygen to his soul. He was enjoying life again but aware at the same time of the colossal problems which lay ahead. The old season may have been grinding to an undistinguished halt but for Redknapp it would signal the start of a cyclonic summer of comings and goings. "I may not be able to get this club into the Premiership but I will give it a damn good go," he said, more in hope it seemed than expectation. "The chairman has spent a lot of money and has nothing to show for it.

Mark Summerbell - Premiership experience.

Financially I don't need to work but this is a challenge I am pleased to accept."

What if Mandaric, tired of costly, pointless and unproductive sackings, had stuck with the personable Rix? Of that Redknapp was never in any doubt: "I am a football man. I like to be out on the training ground with the players, not stuck in an office. That has never been my way. I don't even know what a director of football is supposed to do."

It was in the wake of the Preston defeat, in itself insignificant, that Redknapp revealed that he would have fled his gilded cage in the summer had there been no managerial vacancy at Fratton Park. He was wasting his time, his experience and his vast knowledge of the game - and he knew it. Where he might have gone, not even he knew. As the owner of a new seaside mansion at Sandbanks, near Poole, one of the most expensive pieces of real estate in the country, he was reluctant to uproot. He might have got the job at Leicester before Dave Bassett and Micky Adams took over and even shook hands on it with the Leicester chairman, John Elsom, before changing his mind, while he also spoke to Southampton after Glenn Hoddle had gone. That was the sort of level at which he considered he should be managing. There was no way, he said, he was going back to the lower divisions, trying to make the best of poorer players and small-scale transfers.

He had done that at Bournemouth and at his age and stage there was nothing to be gained from returning to that sort of environment. Had Rix still been in place in the summer, Redknapp said he would have left Fratton Park and taken his chances elsewhere. Mandaric had asked him 15 times to be the manager before accepting. But that was now irrelevant. He was boss at Portsmouth, a club of great potential but small achievement, an outdated ground and a

huge and voluble support; a dynamic and wealthy chairman but large, unwieldy debts and a playing staff made up of players who had largely failed. All this and there were still four matches to go.

Harry - Fifteenth time lucky for Mandaric.

2

REDKNAPP'S REVOLUTION

THE SEASON MAY HAVE BEEN sliding gently towards the oblivion it deserved but there were fixtures to fulfil, players to be signed and dismissed and a rebuilding programme to be organised and put in place. Some 18,020, above average, came to Fratton Park to cast a critical eye over Redknapp's first home appearance as boss, intrigued by the rapid developments of the first few days of the manager's reign. Opponents Burnley had somehow clambered to the verge of the play-offs on the back of a playing staff made up of durable veterans, not the least of whom was Kevin Ball, a key player when namesake Alan took Pompey into the top flight in 1987 but now at 37 in his last season of league football. Redknapp said he did not think Burnley had it about them to go up and so it proved, an uneventful match ending in a 1-1 draw and remarkable only for Todorov's first goal for the club. Judgement was reserved.

For Neil McNab, though, judgement was instantaneous. With Redknapp looking to bring in his own number two, McNab slid out of the back door as the next part in the backroom reorganisation. For more than six months McNab scoured the lower divisions for a new job and got it at Exeter where he became manager, pipping, it was alleged in some quarters, Graham Rix. McNab imported a host of players he had known at Fratton Park such as Lewis Buxton and Carl Pettefer on loan and Scott Hiley, first on loan and then permanently, but it all went wrong in a pitifully short time. Five successive defeats left Exeter floundering at the foot of the third division in late February 2003 and, as the Conference beckoned, the little Scotsman was fired after just five months in charge at St James' Park. This on the same day, incidentally, as another ex-Portsmouth manager, Terry Fenwick, was kicked out by Northampton for failing to win any of his seven-match tenure.

For Pompey fans of an older generation there was sadness at the news in early April of the death of Ike Clarke, the striker who scored the goal which clinched for Portsmouth the

SLEEPING GIANT AWAKES

Neil McNab - judgement day wasn't long in coming.

league championship of 1948-49, the season in which the club so narrowly failed to become the first to record a league and cup double. Only a shock defeat in the FA Cup semi-final by Leicester, then a division below, prevented that feat being accomplished but Pompey won the league again the following year with Clarke playing a prominent part in their success. His death at 87 was not unexpected but it followed quickly the deaths of two other stalwarts of the same era, Ernie Butler and Duggie Reid, men who like Clarke were integral parts of Pompey's glorious past and in their way a constant reminder of how far the club had declined over the following 50 years. Clarke, Butler, Reid and later Peter Harris were part of Portsmouth folklore, were household names beyond Portsea Island in their heyday, and feared and respected at venues such as Old Trafford and Highbury. How many present-day players could claim that? Even to younger fans who had never seen them play, the old-timers were symbolic of a golden era and the ageing personification of a belief that somehow, against present evidence, Pompey were still a "big" club.

Only one of the team Redknapp inherited could be described as great. Robert Prosinecki was the

Robert Prosinecki - Mandaric's gift to Pompey.

chairman's gift to the club, his Balkan links proving vital in persuading the veteran Croatian to spend a year in his footballing dotage on England's south coast. For ten years blond Prosinecki had few to compare with him in world football as a midfield player of vision, skill and sheer class. His free-kicks were legendary and he reached the pinnacle of his career in 1998 when he helped unfancied Croatia take third place in the World Cup. Big clubs fought over his signature and he had the rare distinction of having appeared for both Real Madrid and Barcelona. As Redknapp joked at the time: "He's got the Real Madrid and Barcelona shirts. He just needed one from Pompey for a full house." His signing from the Belgian club, Standard Liege, was quite a coup for Pompey and for Mandaric in particular because he still enjoyed worldwide respect and admiration. He also came with baggage. From Belgium came reports of a reluctant trainer past his best, a moody chain-smoker who was injured more often than he played. But while he was evidently not in his prime, Prosinecki gave Portsmouth a tremendous year of breathtaking close control, sumptuous passing and explosive free-kicks and shots which made the game look pathetically easy. He may not have run around with any enthusiasm, and tackling was an art he was determined not to master, but the effect on Pompey and wary opposition was always apparent. His mere presence added thousands to attendances all around the first division. But now it was decision time. His contract was completed and while Redknapp was among his greatest admirers there were doubts about Prosinecki's desire and ability to play a second full season. Grampus 8, a major club in Japan's J League, opened negotiations and it began to look as if Prosinecki would exercise his right to move on, leaving a big gap in the midfield for Redknapp to fill. How do you replace someone of Prosinecki's calibre?

Prosinecki was one of three Portsmouth players who were preparing for the forthcoming World Cup. Yoshikatsu Kawaguchi was in the Japanese squad and forgotten man Mladen Rudonja was an important part of Slovenia's plans after scoring the goal which took them to the finals for the first time. Prosinecki, in truth, was selected as much on reputation as on form and lasted only the first 45 minutes of Croatia's opening fixture before it became clear that his days as an international performer of the highest quality were over. Rudonja, meanwhile, went to the World Cup but not as a Portsmouth player. In the middle of April he negotiated himself an exit and headed home to pre-

pare for the greatest competition of his life. The story of Rudonja was typical of the way things had gone at Fratton Park in recent years. Nominally he was a Tony Pulis signing from St Truiden but there was never any real evidence that Pulis wanted him, preferring players of a greater

Mladen Rudonja - part of Slovenia's World Cup plans but not of Pompey's.

Above: Tony Pulis - preferred players with greater physical commitment.

physical commitment, and using him only sparingly and when Pulis left, Claridge and Rix had nothing to do with him. Rudonja may have been a national hero in Slovenia after his winning goal against Romania to ensure World Cup qualification, but at Pompey he trained with the reserves and when the reserves had a game, he trained with the youth team. At least in Prosinecki he found someone who understood what he said but he drifted through his two years at Fratton Park, a skilled footballer in the wrong place at the wrong time.

The smiling, ever-popular Kawaguchi brought his own unofficial fan club when Pompey paid £1.8m for him in October 2001; a dedicated, awe-inspired coterie of Japanese journalists who filled the press box at every game he played in, and a few he didn't. Even when Yoshi, as fans called him for convenience' sake, was merely a substitute, there was still a gaggle of his countrymen ready to greet him on the touchline at the final whistle to get his views on a match in which he had not taken any part. The aim of the Kawaguchi signing was simple: To tap into the vast Japanese market and make money. Yoshi was a deity in Japan and his image appeared even on beer mats and adverts for Coca-Cola and McDonalds and the thinking at Fratton Park was that before long every kid in Tokyo would be wearing a replica Pompey shirt. Yoshi was a dedicated trainer, never complained about being so long on the bench and was liked by all who knew him, but he struggled to adapt to the muscular demands of the English first division. In 12 matches he let in 25 goals and was the scapegoat, to some extent, of the Leyton Orient crushing. He did not play again that season and was on the bench again for the whole of 2002-03 once Shaka Hislop had arrived. Pompey told him more than once he could leave but, protected by a long-term and healthy contract, he sat it out. Pompey supporters had a sneaking admiration for him and there

The ever-smiling and ever-popular Yoshikatsu Kawaguchi - in
Japan's World Cup squad but a scapegoat for
the Orient debacle.

was general sympathy, though it was also obvious why Hislop and Dave Beasant - giants in stature by comparison - had been chosen ahead of him. As for the World Cup in his homeland, you've guessed it - he was among the subs.

Even off the field, poor Yoshi had his problems. He was caught speeding near his Fareham home and a warrant was issued for his arrest when he failed to show up for his court case, but the matter was happily resolved in time for him to continue his World Cup preparations. While the finals occupied his mind, Pompey were drawing creditably 1-1 at Birmingham where Courtney Pitt, a Rix signing, scored the goal and then losing at home to Watford 1-0 where all the old deficiencies were strikingly evident. The manager was furious when his players took their traditional lap of honour around the pitch at the final whistle. It was a wonder that any fans had stayed to applaud and as Redknapp said: "I can't believe the players have got the nerve to go out there. What have they got to celebrate? Getting knocked out of the cups by Colchester and Leyton Orient and losing at places like Grimsby?" Redknapp talked also of the long summer ahead, piecing together a team worthy of the Portsmouth name. Talking of Rix, sympathy for him dissipated with the news, never confirmed, of a near £200,000 pay-off in settlement of his contract, yet another money-draining experience for the chairman for whom pay-offs had become a fact of life in his three expensive years at the helm. Rix, disillusioned by his brief spell as manager, resorted to the golf course and an expected link with his old pal Vialli at Watford never materialised and he disappeared altogether when the Italian was sacked.

The final match in another torrid season in the life and chimes of Portsmouth Football Club took place at Manchester City's Maine Road on April 21 with Kevin Keegan's rampaging City already assured of their place among the following season's elite. Redknapp, aware of the enormity of Pompey's task, said all the right things about ruining a promotion party but it was never going to happen and Pompey duly lost 3-1. So it was all over. Fans, directors and the manager all heaved a sigh of relief and now the real business was about to begin in earnest.

As domestic football prepared to close down for 14 weeks for the World Cup finals to take place, and as clubs contemplated the huge loss of the ITV Digital money, Redknapp started his quest to restore Portsmouth towards the sort of grandeur understood by those who from the terraces worshipped Ike Clarke and his teammates half a century before.

There were newspaper reports immediately linking Pompey with Andy Todd of Charlton and big Jamaican striker Ricardo Fuller at Hearts. Redknapp confirmed both were true and in doing so set the tone for the sort of player Pompey were now interested in signing, namely those who had played Premiership football on a regular basis. As it happened, Todd almost joined Pompey but went to Blackburn and Fuller went to Preston where a long-term knee injury ruined his first season. More work was going on behind the scenes, not least in approaching Matthew Taylor, a young left-back at Luton, but more of him later. Meanwhile, Pompey fans, getting used to a revolving door syndrome at Fratton Park, did not know whether to laugh or cry when Paul Gascoigne, his stint at Burnley over, said he would like to play for the club. While there was no disputing Gascoigne's eminence in the English game over the previous decade, or his place as one of the greatest players ever produced by his country, it was also clear that his day was done. Redknapp may have liked the sound of Gazza's enthusiasm but it was a year or two too late and while obscure clubs in Cornwall, north Wales, and even Wessex League's Eastleigh, made publicity-seeking attempts to sign him, he eventually took his chance in China, squeezing the last drop

Paul Gascoigne refuels during Paul Walsh's testimonial game - Pompey fans didn't know whether to laugh or cry when he revealed he wanted to play for the club.

from an incredible talent. Comparisons with Prosinecki were inevitable.

Thomas Thogersen was the last casualty of April 2002. Thogersen made 108 league appearances in four years and came out of the constant turnover of managers better than most in that all rated him. But he was now at the veteran stage and Pompey needed people to leave the club to make way for newcomers. He headed home to Denmark, his task completed, but there were still around 40 players on the club's books at the end of the season and many of those, Redknapp admitted, he had never even seen in meaningful action. More sadly, Rix's son Robbie left the club where he had been a trainee while dad Graham was briefly a candidate for the managerial vacancy at newly-promoted Brighton.

But, as the dust settled, the players dug out the Ambre Solaire and went away to await their destiny; Redknapp, still without an assistant, set about replacing the majority of them. By Christmas 20 of them had gone and by March 2003 another 13 had been signed permanently. Add to them many more players coming and going on loan and there was a big upheaval ahead and plenty of work to be done. 'Arry loved the transfer market but even he had never got involved before on such a grand scale. A quiet summer? You must be joking.

Thomas Thogersen - headed home to Denmark.

NATIONWIDE LEAGUE DIVISION ONE BOTTOM 8 END OF SEASON 2001-02

	P	W	D	L	F	A	Pts
PORTSMOUTH	**46**	**13**	**14**	**19**	**60**	**72**	**53**
Walsall	46	13	12	21	51	71	51
Grimsby Town	46	12	14	20	50	72	50
Sheffield Wed.	46	12	14	20	49	71	50
Rotherham United	46	10	19	17	52	66	49
Crewe Alex.	46	12	13	21	47	76	49
Barnsley	46	11	15	20	59	86	48
Stockport Co.	46	6	8	32	42	102	26

3

HARRY AND JIM

WHAT WOULD HAVE HAPPENED to Pompey if they had succeeded in signing David Ginola? It is a question supporters must have asked themselves time and again over the course of the season as Paul Merson weaved his magic to such telling effect. For a team that had just finished 17th in 2001-02, talk of Pompey and Ginola in the same breath seemed little short of ludicrous. His £35,000 a week wages were enough to give Premiership managers heart palpitations, so to discover, as fans did late in May, that Pompey were interested in signing him, did not make any kind of sense. But with unresolved doubts over Prosinecki's future, this was the sort of crowd-pleasing player in whom Redknapp saw as a possible replacement. The mere fact that informal talks were held suggested Pompey were ready to move on to a whole new plateau. French superstar Ginola, known as much for his lustrous locks as his mazy runs through bewildered defences, had slunk off to France after it was clear he was not David Moyes' type of player at Everton. He awaited new offers, refusing to make concessions to his age and was a little hurt when a queue of interested parties did not form outside his front door. Redknapp reckoned that if Ginola was prepared to admit at 35 that his big pay days were over and to modify his demands, he could prove a massive hit at Fratton Park as Prosinecki's successor. They met and talked and got nowhere. There was money to spend on wages but not the sort he wanted and the move slowly petered out. Ginola waited in vain for what he hoped would be better offers, but they never came and only much later did he sign for Nice, one of Mandaric's former clubs, at a much-reduced salary. If nothing else, the public were now aware of the level of Pompey's ambition and in any case, if Ginola did not want to join Pompey, many others did.

One of the problems facing Redknapp was that at the end of the season only a handful of players were out of contract so a clearout was not an option, or at least not one that did not involve pay-offs. Justin Edinburgh announced his retirement after failing to overcome an ankle injury but only Stefani Miglioranzi, Ben Griffiths and Garry Brady had committed the cardinal sin, in a

After a long career and failing to overcome an ankle injury, exit Justin Edinburgh.

close season of mass footballer redundancies, of running out of contract. Redknapp was fair to Miglioranzi, the Brazilian-born American of Italian extraction, and Brady, and gave them a chance to stake a claim for new contracts by playing them in some of the last five games. Miglioranzi even impressed him in a sweeper role, but there was no reprieve. Players had to go. It was as simple as that.

Looking through the list of contracted players, Redknapp must have wondered how to move on those he did not want. Such was his disdain for most of them that only a handful - Gary O'Neil, Nigel Quashie, Linvoy Primus, Kevin Harper and Jason Crowe - were to feature regularly in the season ahead. He wanted a whole new team, a whole new coaching set-up and if Ginola did not want to jump aboard, others were not so reluctant once it became clear that for the first time in many years Pompey were ambitious to do something more positive than simply survive in the first division.

Reminders of Portsmouth's dim past were never far away. They were obliged to pay Lindsay Parsons, Pulis's number two, £36,000 in compensation and the club were called to the Football Association to explain their poor disciplinary record. It was the worst collection of red and yellow cards in the country bar none and Pompey knew they had been fortunate to escape with a £30,000 suspended fine. It could have been far more damaging. Old jokes about more cards than points and about Pompey being useless and dirty were never far from the surface as black-humoured fans discussed the past, but it was not a subject for laughter in the corridors of power at Fratton Park. Pompey needed a boost to its image and its self-esteem, and discipline did improve almost overnight so that by March 2003 not a single player had been sent off. Mid-season suspensions for Quashie, De Zeeuw, Diabate and Taylor were all as a result of accumulating five bookings rather than for serious misdemeanours. The competitive edge was not impaired or compromised but the manager made it clear banned players were of no use to the promotion cause.

So, as the nation settled to watch matches on the other side of the world, Pompey got down to the business of recruitment on a scale never before experienced or even envisaged. There was talk of Leicester's Andy Impey, of the Cameroonian Raymond Kalla and of Middlesbrough's Robbie Mustoe. There were rumours of Wigan's Arjan De Zeeuw and Manchester United's Ronnie Wallwork. What to believe? Yet all this against a background of strange quietness elsewhere and, as the summer wore on, Pompey's name became linked with more players than any other at any level. Other clubs had simply shut up shop. Admittedly, not much transfer activity was expected in May while holidaying players were still under contract, or in June while the World Cup was in full flow, but even as the new season approached the transfer market seemed curiously dead. Paralysed by the ITV Digital fiasco, Pompey's first division rivals decided virtually en bloc to offload those players whose wages they could not afford and not to replace them. This provided a wonderful opportunity for Pompey. Redknapp had money, by no means a colossal amount, and no other club appeared to have any. Relegated clubs Leicester, Ipswich and Derby - all rightly fancied as promotion contenders - froze at the loss of the Premiership's smooth-flowing gravy train and found themselves burdened by individual wage bills hopelessly at odds with first division budgets. All three were to endure the humiliation of going into financial administration, their Premiership parachute money next-to-useless in their straightened new circumstances. Here was a big chance, then, and Redknapp was just the man to exploit it.

The first to come aboard HMS Pompey was Hayden Foxe, the red-headed Australian on whose behalf Redknapp had fought long and hard to obtain a work permit when at West Ham. Like Todorov, Foxe had fallen by the wayside at Upton Park under new management and once a basic £400,000 fee had been agreed the rest was a formality, the player signing on his way to Heathrow and a holiday Down Under. One down, many more to go. Scott Wilson was another target after his successful loan but it was a move which never developed, Redknapp having made defensive solidity a priority in his team-building. Wilson ended up at Dunfermline and so the search continued elsewhere. Meanwhile, rumours continued: Paul Evans of Brentford, Nottingham Forest's Jim Brennan, Fritz Emeron of Bordeaux and, over two or three spectacular days, even the world-class Brazilian Romario got a mention in the newspapers. It may never have got anywhere near happen-

The Ginger Foxe - Australian Hayden was the first aboard Redknapp's re-fitted HMS Pompey.

Within the space of 24 hours Redknapp surprised everyone with the signings of (from top left clockwise) Arjan De Zeeuw, Vincent Pericard, Richard Hughes and Matt Taylor.

ing but it served its purpose in making clear to English domestic football at large that Pompey were a club on the up and chasing players of international renown.

Cagey Redknapp was keeping the identity of the players he really wanted a closely-guarded secret, so it was a major surprise on June 5 when the signings of Richard Hughes, Matt Taylor and Vincent Pericard were announced simultaneously, followed 24 hours later by that of De Zeeuw. All, except injured Scottish under-21 international Hughes, were to make significant contributions to the magnificent campaign ahead. Hughes was out of contract at Bournemouth and was a close friend of Howe. He needed no convincing that Fratton Park was the place to be. Bournemouth muttered about only receiving £100,000 for a junior international but the Italian-speaking Hughes was contemplating a return to the country in which he was raised. Had that been the case Bournemouth would have got nothing. Pericard was an unknown. The Cameroonian-born Frenchman was sent to Portsmouth on loan by Juventus and the gangling, dreadlocked newcomer looked awkward and ill-at-ease at first to the extent that Redknapp admitted to thinking he might have made a mistake. But once he had come to terms with the physical

endeavour required and put away fine goals against Forest, Wimbledon and Bradford, Pericard settled to become a key squad player. But of those three, the rangy Taylor was the most interesting and, as it turned out, the most spectacular.

Hints at what sort of player Taylor, then 20, might become were offered by angry Joe Kinnear, the Luton manager, who was baffled that he had chosen Portsmouth ahead of Premiership interest from Spurs and Sunderland. Taylor was out of contract at Luton, who had just won promotion to the second division. Taking advantage of his freedom, the left wing-back had signed for Pompey in the belief that he was not yet ready for the top flight. He said he preferred a season or two in the first division to sitting on a Premiership bench. "At least Dick Turpin wore a mask," spluttered disbelieving Kinnear as he contemplated Harry's highway robbery. "He's nicked the best left-back in the country." Indeed, Pompey only offered £100,000, on the basis that Kinnear's fury would lead to a transfer tribunal - and so it proved. Eventually Pompey were ordered to pay a fee rising to £750,000, well short of Luton's £1.5m valuation. It would not be long before Taylor began to make a mockery of such a fee, prompting Paul Merson to compare him with Roberto Carlos and to place him in the £8m category, proclaiming him to be better than Ashley Cole and Wayne Bridge as England left-backs. Taylor was a phenomenon, marauding down the left with pace, athleticism and sheer determination and causing Premiership clubs to question their scouting systems. How had they missed him? Uncompromising Dutchman De Zeeuw had tasted the Premiership at Barnsley, briefly, and had spent the last three years at Wigan in the second division. Big, strong and reliable, De Zeeuw was wanted by Reading and Birmingham but saw the possibilities at Portsmouth and was quickly persuaded by Redknapp that this was the right move for him.

While all of those were important in the year ahead, it is fair to say that the Pompey public were not dancing in the streets with joy. De Zeeuw was in his 33rd year, no one had heard of Pericard, Taylor had been playing in the third division and Hughes, when fit, had done nothing to stop Bournemouth going down. Luton, Bournemouth and Wigan were not the sort of clubs from which first division champions were discovered and produced.

At least everyone knew of Shaka Hislop, the giant Trinidadian surplus to requirements at West Ham where David James had become first choice. Shaka was out of contract and unsure that it was a good move

stepping down to the first division, especially to a club like Pompey with a poor record in recent years. Redknapp had signed him for West Ham from Newcastle so there was a bond already in place. Wolves were said to be keen but Hislop gradually came round to the idea, propagated by Redknapp, that something extraordinary was about to happen on the south coast in Portsmouth's footballing backwater.

There was more transfer activity taking place even as Hislop was putting pen to paper. Alessandro Zamperini, he of the smouldering Latin looks, headed home to Modena and his mother's cooking. Zamperini, who had food parcels sent to him by his anxious Mama during his year in Portsmouth, was not sure there was a place for him in the new Pompey and left. At the same time, Wolves' Welsh international midfield player Carl Robinson signed on a three-month trial after failing a medical. Robinson proved his fitness, signed a three-year contract, and was then sent out on loan to Sheffield Wednesday and Walsall. Very peculiar. Manchester United's Wallwork, meanwhile, was signing for West Brom in preference to Pompey. Redknapp was still not finished, organising a week's trial for Dele Adebola, released by Birmingham, and making it clear that Fabrizio Ravanelli's £40,000 a week wages at Derby

OUT: Alessandro Zamperini - smouldering Italian looks, but a penchant for his mother's cooking.

IN: Shaka Hislop - another former Redknapp man at West Ham, signed for Pompey instead of Wolves.

were not necessarily a problem if Derby were willing to pay 75 per cent of them and let him play for Pompey. The Ravanelli-for-Pompey saga rumbled on through the

season and never got close to resolution, but it was always a source of interest for fans of both clubs. Adebola did not last, heading for Crystal Palace and

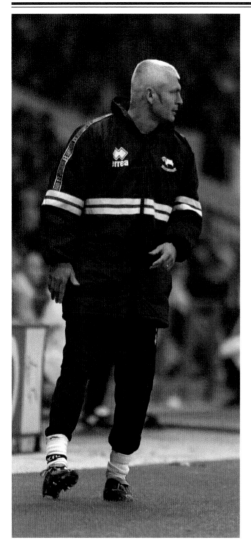

Fabrizio Ravanelli - the "will he, won't he" saga ran and ran.

was a move which suited both parties, though it has to be said that Derry was one of the better players inherited by Redknapp, as he acknowledged.

There was one yawning chasm in the Portsmouth of 2002-03 as the new season loomed on the horizon. There was no assistant manager. Indeed, the backroom staff was still being reorganised. Mark O'Connor had escaped the purge and it helped that Redknapp knew him from their Bournemouth days together. O'Connor ran the youth team, Andy Awford took over the reserves and scouted opponents, and Pompey legend Alan Knight stayed on as goalkeeping coach. There was also no first team coach. Before long Kevin Bond, Alan Ball's assistant, was back at Fratton Park to fill that vacancy. Redknapp and Bond went back a long way. This gets complicated: Harry played at Bournemouth for Kevin's dad, John. Later, when Harry became boss at Bournemouth he signed Kevin to play in his defence. Got it?

But that had still not solved the problem of Redknapp's assistant. So it was with universal delight when it became apparent that Jim Smith was returning to Pompey as director of football, but with a much more involved role than that title implies. Smith was one of football's great survivors, seeing off intimidating, despotic chairmen such as Rob-

being joined there in a £400,000 deal by Shaun Derry, the powerful midfield player who had led a player-deputation to the chairman pleading for Rix to keep his job. When that failed, and with Rix now history, he preferred to take his chances elsewhere. It ert Maxwell and Jim Gregory to put together a managerial career which over 35 years took him on a tour of England to such clubs as Boston, Blackburn, Birmingham, Newcastle, Oxford, Queen's Park Rangers and, of course, Pompey. Smith so nearly brought FA Cup glory to Fratton Park in 1992, building a team of young talents, such as Awford and Darren Anderton, before it was ruthlessly cut away from him to raise cash. He left in 1995 and spent six years at Derby in the Premiership before impending relegation cost him his job, and a director of football spell at Coventry did not last long. At 61, Jim was out of a job and wondering if there would ever be a niche in football again. The game had been his life. Away on holiday in Spain, Jim got the call to join Harry's crusade at Fratton Park. It sounded too good to be true; the chance to round off some unfinished business. His return to England was hit by an airport strike but it was the only, temporary, setback and on June 26 the second coming of the Bald Eagle was announced at the same time as the signing of Hislop. For Pompey fans it was a dream team come true and provided real hope for the year ahead. Redknapp and Smith, mutually respectful, had been opponents for many years at different clubs. Now they were colleagues with one single aim: To get Pompey into the big time.

Kevin Bond - another of Redknapp's Bournemouth connections.

Within weeks their unification was the subject of a terrace chant, based on the children's programme, "Rosie and Jim".

Altogether now....Harry and Jim....Harry and Jim....Harry and Jim....Harry and Jim.

Altogether now….Harry and Jim….Harry and Jim….
Harry and Jim….Harry and Jim.

4

MERSON ARRIVES

ALL THROUGH THE LATTER part of the build-up to the new season there were growing rumours that, with David Ginola no longer a target and Robert Prosinecki heading home to the Balkans, Pompey were pursuing another big name. From the Midlands it became apparent that Paul Merson and Aston Villa had fallen out in a very big way. Merson had been selected sparingly by Graham Taylor the previous season and then it became clear that Taylor would be using the former Arsenal and England player only occasionally, as a substitute, in the year ahead. Protected by a contract worth at least £20,000 a week, Merson could have accepted his fate, sat back and collected his money. Instead, Merson's pride was badly hurt. In effect, a man as eminent in the game as Taylor had told him his 16-year career as a vital, top-flight player was over. Although he had not said as much, Taylor did not want him.

By the start of August Pompey were well on the way to giving him a fresh chance in the first division, negotiations concluding

Paul Merson - Pompey's latest acquisition.

quickly and ending in a press conference at Fratton Park to announce his signing five days before the season was due to begin.

Opinions in and around Portsmouth were distinctly divided. On the one hand, here was an international player with a tremendous pedigree and with skill unlikely to be rivalled elsewhere in Pompey's division. On

SLEEPING GIANT AWAKES

Merson signs - "I have not come here as a soft option."

the other hand, here was a 34-year old, perhaps past his best, perhaps carrying too much baggage (of all kinds) and perhaps using Pompey as a last rest home before retirement. Who was wrong: Taylor or Redknapp? So keen to dispense with Merson was Taylor that no fee was involved and Villa readily agreed to pay what amounted to half his wages simply to get rid of him. For Redknapp, a keen punter, it was a colossal gamble. Merson could have been a huge £10,000 a week failure.

But the signs were good at the press conference. Unable to contain his fury at Taylor's treatment of him, he accused Villa of lacking ambition. More to the point, he vowed to become the driving force behind what he believed would be a promotion campaign. "I have not come here as a soft option," he said. "I believe this club can get into the Premiership this season. I can see the ambition in the manager and the chairman and there is no other club outside the Premiership I would have joined." All pleasantly reassuring, but the new season was upon us and Merson had a matter of four or five training sessions to hone his fitness, acquaint himself with his new teammates and prepare physically and mentally for the task ahead. If he could also stick two fingers in the air in Taylor's direction then so be it.

MERSON ARRIVES

Pre-season is always a tricky time. Managers tend to play down the significance of friendlies if their team loses, and talk of a golden future when they win. So, what to make of Pompey's summer? A summer which in fact began as far back as July 10 when Celtic came to Fratton Park, bringing with them a horde of green and white-clad fans who filled the Milton End as no other team's supporters were to do in the year ahead and swelling the crowd to an unprecedented 11,553. Redknapp used 21 players, De Zeeuw was carried off on a stretcher after colliding with Howe and there were chances for trialists Didier Ernst and Drees Bourchaart; chances not taken.

Richard Hughes and Linvoy Primus scored the goals in a boring 3-2 defeat. Redknapp travelled to Bognor three days later where a line-up made up mainly of the previous season's first team confirmed his worst fears about them in a scrappy 1-0 win over Ryman League part-timers. Vincent Pericard scored the goal.

And then it was off to the West Country where Redknapp's new squad stayed at Nigel Mansell's country club. Previous managers had presided over defeats at places like Dorchester and Yeovil, blaming poor pitches, over-exuberant opponents and on one memorable occasion Terry Fenwick said his players were "too fit". This time there

Celtic at Fratton Park - a sign of things to come?

was only good news. Newquay were seen off as they should have been, 5-0, with Pericard, Todorov, Tiler and Harper (2) getting the goals, the scoreline meaningless in itself because of the standard of the opposition. But the 4-1 win at Torquay, later to be promotion candidates in the third division, was regarded as much more important because it was against full-time professionals. Ukrainian Sergiy Konovalov, who played against Newquay in a bid to earn a contract, scored one of the goals in front of 1,420 at Plainmoor. Foxe, Todorov and Pitt got the others. Mark Burchill scored the Pompey goal in a 1-1 draw at Conference club Farnborough, but the real test of the gelling power of the new Pompey came when Chelsea visited Fratton Park on July 27. Some 10,000, intrigued by the opposition and by Redknapp's hastily-arranged squad, also got a look at trialist Dele Adebola, in what proved to be his only Pompey showing, and Frenchman Frederic Brando. Chelsea won 3-1 with Pericard scoring for Pompey and Lampard, Oliveira and Huth replying. Judgement was reserved, bearing in mind Chelsea's class. The reserves, meanwhile, overcame Dr Marten's League Weymouth and Havant to complete a generally encouraging pre-season. All that remained before hostilities began was a prestigious home friendly on August 3 with Spaniards Alaves.

Pericard - on target against Bognor, Newquay and Chelsea.

A crowd of 3,301 saw Rory Allen get Pompey's goal in a 1-1 draw with a superb header following good work down the left by Hughes and Taylor. More on the Strange Case of Rory Allen later, but the performance of the team against talented and sophisticated opponents was most encouraging for the new management team of Redknapp, Smith and Bond. Not a bad result at all.

Robert Prosinecki concluded the preparations by announcing that he had left Pompey after all.

MERSON ARRIVES

Those who had marvelled at his fantastic skills realised they had been lucky to see him at all in a Pompey shirt. The hunched, scowling Croatian, likened more than once in the national newspapers to Albert Steptoe, had enjoyed his year in England and it was never going to be a long-term arrangement. He had his critics for his apparent refusal to break sweat, but the majority of supporters knew they had been given an unexpected taste of the exotic and were happy to overlook his shortcomings. After his move to Japan collapsed over terms, Prosinecki announced that he might return to Croatia to start a sports paper but settled for one last season in Slovenia, with Mladen Rudonja as it happened, at Olimpiana Lublijana.

Expectation and excitement grew in the days after Merson's signing. Season ticket sales received a welcome boost though interest at that stage was a trickle compared with what was to follow later. As Pompey stormed towards the championship, a tidal wave of support took hold so that beyond Christmas some 15,000 had bought season tickets among a capacity attendance of around 19,500. Peter Storrie and Paul Weld chuckled with delight. But that was the future. The mood going into the first fixture at home to Nottingham Forest was buoyant but cautious; the fear of hoping for too much tempering a tingling feeling that here was a brand new team on the threshold of something great. A streak of Pompey pessimism, borne of consistent setbacks and failure over 50 years, was never far from conversations. "False dawn" was a key phrase. This was reinforced with

Rory Allen - a goal against Alaves but injury hoodoo struck again.

the late news that injury would prevent Courtney Pitt playing at all during the first month and that Rory Allen was injured - yet again. Just when it seemed he had beaten an injury hoodoo stretching back three years he dropped out on the eve of the season, leaving a none-too-pleased Redknapp with some 24 hours to find and groom a replacement. Allen's impressive form in pre-season matches led to Redknapp putting his name down on the team-sheet for the Forest visit, so his late withdrawal came as a bitter blow.

Jim Smith came to the rescue, recommending to Redknapp the Derby striker Deon Burton. Derby were already feeling the financial pinch after relegation and anxious to get rid of high-earning players, even at this eleventh hour. Burton may not have been in the Ravanelli wage class but John Gregory, the former Portsmouth manager, was happy to let him go out on loan. For Burton it was a homecoming. Raised in Reading, he joined Pompey as an apprentice in the days when school-leaving youths were apprentices, not "trainees" or "scholars". Burton made his Pompey debut as a 16-year old and after scoring some critical goals, not least a relegation-averting last-day winner at Huddersfield, he was sold to Derby for £1.5m. Burton had his moments in the Premiership and in the process was selected to play for his national team, Jamaica, earning a place in their 1998 World Cup squad and being named at the expense of such great sporting figures as Courtney Walsh and Merlene Ottey as the Caribbean island's sports personality of the year. Burton rushed south, signed the forms and took his place in the team to face Forest. As a rallying call on the day before the season began, Redknapp promised to end years of misery for the long-suffering Portsmouth public: "We may not get automatic promotion," he said, "and it may take a time for the players to get to know each other, but I feel we can chase a play-off place at the very least." Heartening words indeed, but would they be borne out in the long season about to unfurl before him?

Saturday, August 10

PORTSMOUTH 2
NOTTINGHAM FOREST 0

Here it was at last: the big day. Forest had tricky, pacy David Johnson up front and a young and talented team so that in many ways it was the perfect test of the new-look Pompey. Eddie Howe collapsed in agony after five minutes, went off after eight with a dislocated knee and was to play no further part in the season. Typical, muttered the disbelievers, it's all going wrong

MERSON ARRIVES

**Deon Burton - return to Portsmouth
a homecoming, and a goal on debut.**

already. Redknapp introduced seven new players for their debut (Howe was making his first home start) and only O'Neil, Quashie and Primus remained of the old, discredited guard. As Howe was taken on a stretcher to the dressing room, Burton marked his return with a goal. Pericard's spectacular diving header just before half-time ensured the very best of starts to the new campaign. Forest, and Johnson, rarely threatened.

Portsmouth (3-4-1-2): Hislop; Howe (Primus 9), Foxe, De Zeeuw; O'Neil, Robinson, Quashie, Taylor; Merson; Burton, Pericard.
Subs (not used): Kawaguchi, Crowe, Barrett, Burchill.
Goals: Burton (8), Pericard (45).
Booked: Foxe, Quashie.
Nottingham Forest (4-5-1): Ward; Thompson (Harewood 45), Hall, Hjelde, Walker; Louis-Jean, Williams, Scimeca, Prutton, Brennan (Lester 50); Johnson.
Subs (not used): Roche, Reid, Westcarr.
Booked: Prutton, Hjelde.
Attendance: 18,910.
Referee: D Gallagher (Oxfordshire).

Harry Redknapp, delighted by the start, noted how the newcomers had bedded down so quickly. There were some tough matches to come, he said, but this was a good start against a capable team who, he pointed out, would press for promotion in the fullness of time. So it proved. Redknapp, meanwhile, was not deceived into thinking that his list of signings had been completed. Two days later his club were linked with Dennis Wise, the errant former England midfield player, who had been sacked by Leicester after breaking a teammate's jaw over a game of cards. Wise was never short of talent but his fiery reputation meant that Pompey were one of very few clubs who showed an interest. It was an interest which did not develop and he later pitched up at Millwall.

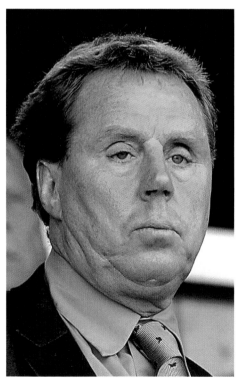

Redknapp - delighted by the start made by his new-look team.

Tuesday, August 13

SHEFFIELD UNITED 1
PORTSMOUTH 1

At the time Pompey were just thankful to end a run of nine successive defeats at Bramall Lane. United were later to have a tremendous season of their own in league and cups, so in context it was a valuable and important point gained. Wearing their new gold away strip, Pompey fell behind early on when Peter Ndlovu seized on a Taylor error to beat Shaka Hislop from 25 yards with a rising drive. But there was a resilience about Pompey's performance, and where in previous years they might have capitulated, they fought back to equalise when Burton ran on to a Merson trademark flick to round Kenny before scoring. Pompey were not just happy to equalise. Later in the match, with Sheffield United on the defensive, Taylor, Burton and Merson all missed chances for a winner.

Sheffield United (4-4-2): Kenny; Kozluk, Ullathorne (Doane 45), Yates, Murphy; Brown, Ndlovu (McGovern 67), Jagielka, Tonge (McCall 79); Asaba, Onuora.
Subs (not used): Javary, Peschisolido.
Goals: Ndlovu (12)
Booked: Tonge.
Portsmouth (3-5-2): Hislop; Primus, Foxe, De Zeeuw; O'Neil, Robinson (Hughes 74), Quashie, Merson, Taylor; Burton (Burchill 90), Pericard (Todorov 68).
Subs (not used): Kawaguchi, Crowe.
Goals: Burton (25)

MERSON ARRIVES

Booked: Taylor, Burton, Merson.
Attendance: 16,093.
Referee: A Bates (Staffordshire).

Ipswich striker Marcus Stewart was the surprise new name to be linked with Pompey. By now Redknapp had sensed that relegated clubs - and a few in the Premiership who had not been relegated - were in the business of shedding players. Like Derby and Leicester, Ipswich were finding life in the first division very difficult. Big wages, no money to pay them. Stewart had made a reputation at Bristol Rovers and Huddersfield as a high class finisher, a reputation he carried with him to Ipswich but he man-

aged only six in 2001-02 as George Burley's team slid into the first division to general surprise. Redknapp made it clear that he would be prepared to sign Stewart if Ipswich in effect shared his salary but, like that of Wise, it was a move which did not develop. Later Stewart moved to Sunderland where his famed goalscoring ability completely deserted him. Meanwhile, the build-up for the visit to Crystal Palace was given added spice by former Pompey favourite Shaun Derry's presence in the opposition ranks.

Saturday, August 17

CRYSTAL PALACE 2
PORTSMOUTH 3

Shaun Derry - his appearance in the Palace ranks added spice to the occasion.

Derry lasted 73 minutes and could do nothing to stop Pompey's incredible revival from two goals down. Dougie Freedman and Tony Popovic with a header gave Palace a deserved half time lead and there was talk of bubbles bursting. Danny Butterfield also struck a post before Pompey at last got themselves together. Hayden Foxe headed in Taylor's corner in the 68th minute and suddenly Palace fell apart. Pompey's match-winner came in the unlikely shape of Jason Crowe, the former Arsenal junior who came on at half time as a substitute. Crowe had managed only one in three years for Pompey. Here he scored twice in three minutes to stun Selhurst Park and delight the 4,000 travelling fans. Getting fitter by the match, Merson was at the hub of all the best moves.

Crystal Palace (3-5-2): Clarke; Powell (Austin 21), Popovic, Mullins; Butterfield, Thomson (Kabba 78), Derry (Fleming 73), Riihilahti, Granville; Adebola, Freedman.
Subs (not used): Kolinko, Black.
Goals: Freedman (40), Popovic (42).
Portsmouth (3-5-2): Hislop; Primus, Foxe, De Zeeuw; O'Neil (Crowe 45), Robinson (Hughes 45), Quashie, Merson, Taylor; Burton, Pericard (Todorov 22).
Subs (not used): Kawaguchi, Burchill.
Goals: Foxe (68), Crowe (69, 72).
Booked: De Zeeuw, Primus.
Attendance: 18,315.
Referee: S Dunn (Bristol).

Gianluca Festa - six years of Premiership experience at Middlesbrough.

The public appetite whetted by a most encouraging start to the season, Redknapp signalled intentions by making it known that Pompey were keen to sign Tim Sherwood of Tottenham (reserves), while free agent Moreno Toricelli, late of bankrupt Fiorentina, headed to England for a week on trial with Pompey. It was to be another six long months before Sherwood was to escape Glenn Hoddle and White Hart Lane where he was clearly no longer needed, but financial negotiations were always delicate. Toricelli showed his quality in training, talked to other English clubs, but eventually returned to Italy without signing. At the same time Pompey announced that the luckless Allen was to have his eighth operation in three years, another setback in a Pompey career which somehow refused to start. Not that Redknapp had time to dwell on his latest setback. He was busy talking to Gianluca Festa, the 33-year old Italian defender, a player of vast experience and a background which included Inter Milan and six years in the Premiership at Middlesbrough. Steve McClaren, in a move reminiscent of the events surrounding Merson's transfer but without the acrimony, said Festa was not going to be a regular in the season ahead and, like Villa, was prepared to pay half his wages. Pompey had a proven, footballing, high-cali-bre signing for around £10,000 a week. Concerned by Howe's injury, Festa was the perfect replacement and, in time, with De Zeeuw, Foxe and Primus, formed a formidable barrier which was breached only occasionally. There was further good news when chairman Mandaric, his enthusiasm restored by the uplifting start to the season, promised more funds would be available for further newcomers.

Saturday, August 24

PORTSMOUTH 3
WATFORD 0

Merson murdered Watford almost single-handedly with a vintage performance. He was involved in everything Pompey created, having a shot cleared off the line before sending Crowe scuttling into the area where he was fouled by Marcus Gayle. Merson put away the resulting spot-kick and Watford never recovered. In first half stoppage time, Merson was at it again, setting Burton free down the right. Todorov was perfectly placed to turn in Burton's low cross. Two minutes after the break, Todorov returned the compliment, putting in Burton to score with a left foot shot. Watford hung on grimly. Merson hit the bar and to complete their misery Allan Nielsen was sent off for dissent in the closing stages. It was all too late by then. Festa cruised through his debut, looking as assured as expected.

Portsmouth (3-4-1-2): Hislop; Festa, Foxe, De Zeeuw; Crowe, Hughes (C. Robinson 83), Quashie, Taylor; Merson (O'Neil 80); Burton (Burchill 75), Todorov.
Subs (not used): Kawaguchi, Primus.
Goals: Merson (pen, 42), Todorov (45), Burton (47).

Watford (3-5-2): Chamberlain; Cox, Dyche, Gayle; Ardley (Doyley 76), P. Robinson, Nielsen, Hyde, Hand (Vernazza 52); Smith (Glass 80), Webber.
Subs (not used): Lee, Foley.
Booked: Cox, Hand, Hyde, Nielsen.
Sent off: Nielsen (79).
Attendance: 17,901
Referee: M Cooper (West Midlands).

Merson - top billing against Watford and a goal from the penalty spot to open his Pompey account.

MERSON ARRIVES

Two days later, August Bank Holiday Monday, Pompey were off to Grimsby, never an easy team to subdue, and in recent seasons traditional rivals of Pompey at the foot of the table. This time the gap in class was quickly apparent although the margin of victory was narrow and achieved with only five minutes to spare.

Monday, August 26

GRIMSBY TOWN 0
PORTSMOUTH 1

Gillingham it was who led the table in the early weeks but the win at Grimsby took Pompey to the top in their place and they never lost it. Predictably, Grimsby made Pompey work for their win. Indeed it was Grimsby who enjoyed most of the possession and most of the pressure. Pompey looked dangerous on the break with Coyne denying Burton and Taylor (Deon and Matt, not Richard and Liz). Burchill replaced Burton after 58 minutes and with five minutes remaining it was the former Scottish international, recovering from a year out of action with cruciate ligament damage, who raced on to Todorov's flick from Hislop's long clearance, turned his marker and cracked in a 20 yard left foot shot. It was his first goal since recovering and his joy matched that of the travelling fans.

Mark Burchill - the former Scottish international came on for Burton and scored the winning goal.

Grimsby (4-5-1): Coyne; McDermott, Gallimore, Ford, Chettle; Campbell, Cooke, Caldicott (P. Robinson 87), Groves, Barnard (Rowan 87); Kabba.
Subs (not used): Ward, B. Hughes, Bolder.
Booked: Kabba, Barnard, Groves.
Portsmouth (3-4-1-2): Hislop; Festa, Foxe, De Zeeuw; Crowe (Harper 63), R Hughes, Quashie, Taylor; Merson; Burton (Burchill 58), Todorov (C. Robinson 89).
Subs (not used): Kawaguchi, Primus.
Goals: Burchill (85)
Booked: Todorov, De Zeeuw, Hislop, Harper.
Attendance: 5,770.
Referee: M Messias (North Yorkshire).

Brighton had stormed through the lower divisions, winning the second and third division championships in successive seasons. With much the same squad, ace goalscorer Bobby Zamora injured and a summer of procrastination over a new manager, local rivals Albion were not finding life in the higher division as easy. Portsmouth-based Shaun Wilkinson, a former Pompey schoolboy, hoped to be in the Brighton team to face his home city club, at the same time hoping Pompey would win promotion. Divided loyalties? Not a bit of it. But he got less than 20 minutes as a substitute, happy not with the result but with having played at his beloved Fratton Park.

Saturday, August 31

PORTSMOUTH 4
BRIGHTON 2

Struggling Brighton even led 2-1 before Pompey belatedly regained their equilibrium and took control. Matt Taylor put Pompey ahead but there were shocks in store. Danny Cullip took advantage of a ricochet to equalise and then a Richard Hughes error was seized on by Paul Brooker. Leaders Pompey were in trouble, or were they? Former Pompey defender Guy Butters controversially fouled Burton and Merson scored from the spot. Perhaps a little lucky, but who cares? On such incidents are championships won and lost. Andy Petterson, another ex-Pompey man, kept out Todorov and Crowe before Taylor set up Todorov just before the break. That goalscoring discovery Crowe banged in another after 52 minutes and there was no way back this time for Brighton. Their misery was compounded when Barrett was sent off after a clash with Taylor. Three more points and Pompey were never at their best.

Portsmouth (3-4-1-2): Hislop; Festa, Foxe, De Zeeuw; Crowe (Harper 66), Hughes, Quashie, Taylor; Merson; Burton (Burchill 66), Todorov (Robinson 85).
Subs (not used): Kawaguchi, Primus.
Goals: Taylor (3), Merson (pen, 26),

Matt Taylor celebrates his opener and his first for the club.

MERSON ARRIVES

Todorov slides home the goal that takes the lead against Brighton - the first of many in 2002-03 for this skilled finisher.

Todorov (45), Crowe (52).
Booked: Hughes, Foxe, Quashie, Taylor.
Brighton (4-5-1): Petterson; Pethick, Cullip, Butters, Watson; Marney, Carpenter, Oatway, Melton (Wilkinson 72), Brooker; Barrett.
Subs (not used): Packham, Rogers, Jones, Hinshelwood.
Goals: Cullip (9), Brooker (19).
Booked: Cullip, Butters, Oatway, Wilkinson.
Sent off: Barrett (76).
Attendance: 19,031
Referee: S Bennett (Kent).

TOP 6 AT END OF AUGUST 2002

	P	W	D	L	F	A	Pts
PORTSMOUTH	6	5	1	0	14	5	16
Norwich City	6	4	2	0	13	2	14
Leicester City	6	4	1	1	8	7	13
Wolverhampton Wdrs	6	3	2	1	14	7	11
Rotherham United	6	3	2	1	13	7	11
Coventry City	5	3	1	1	7	7	10

So the month ended with Pompey top and unbeaten. There was a growing belief among all concerned that with August now gone Pompey were capable of becoming promotion contenders. How genuine their challenge, the following months would show. But so far, as the summer came to an end, so good.

5

"YOU CAN'T WIN 'EM ALL"

HARRY REDKNAPP WAS NAMED Nationwide Manager of the Month for the first division for August as Pompey sat contentedly at the top of the table, unbeaten. There was no other candidate and where some managers dedicate such awards to their players, Redknapp mentioned only one: Paul Merson. Not that he underestimated the contributions made by others, it was just that Merson's awesome skill and his commitment to the Pompey cause stood out above all others. "Merse has been tremendous ever since he came here. He's a different class," said Redknapp, delighted that his star signing was already delivering. "Some people might have thought he was coming down here to retire but he has proved to be a great captain and leader on and off the pitch. Paul is as enthusiastic as he has ever been in his career and is loving every minute of it at Fratton Park. He is a great influence on the younger players and one of the main reasons why we have started so well."

Merson was relishing it. Freed from his troubles at Villa Park and also from the injuries which interrupted his last season there, he was finding the first division well within his reduced capabilities. He may not now have been capable of covering every blade of grass, but there was not a player with a more profound influence.

Paul Merson - "He's a different class," said Redknapp.

"YOU CAN'T WIN 'EM ALL"

Gary O'Neil - making a big impression at Pompey and selected for the England under-21 squad.

Not that Merson was the only player to have caught the eye. The surging runs of Taylor and the precocious midfield skills of O'Neil had earned recognition at a higher level. The Football Association agreed to lay on a chauffeur-driven car to take them from Bolton, where England were playing Yugoslavia on the Friday night, south to Gillingham where Pompey were playing next day in a first division fixture. Redknapp said: "The FA have agreed to bring them to our hotel and even if they do play for the under-21s neither of them will have a problem playing for us as well. Matty will run and run all day long. We put him through a fitness test and he came out as an elite athlete, so he can handle it. We could have called the game off because Carl Robinson is also away on international duty with Wales but I don't want to start cancelling games the way we are playing at the moment. We don't want to have to go to Gillingham in the middle of winter so the game goes ahead regardless."

As it happened, neither did play at the Reebok but it was a timely recognition that Pompey were not a one-man band. Young O'Neil, 19, was already making a big impression for Pompey. This was already his fourth season and Redknapp had expressed surprise that no Premiership club was showing more than a passing interest in him. Sunderland and Celtic had been linked in pre-Redknapp days but Pompey were under no pressure to sell, the chairman was swift to emphasise.

Contrast his youthful promise to Dave Beasant, who was almost 25 when O'Neil first saw the light of day in south London. Beasant had done a thoroughly efficient job with Pompey, belying his age and fending off the challenge of Kawaguchi, among others, to remain Pompey's number one goalkeeper under Rix. Now, with Hislop as first choice

Dave Beasant - the oldest player in the Football League, but now surplus to requirements at Pompey.

Beasant was not a man to dwell on the past. Time may have been running out but he still wanted to be playing regularly. When it became clear that there was no room for him at Pompey, he was off. There was a suggestion he might have stayed as goalkeeping coach but once that possibility collapsed, Beasant was away on a nationwide tour that took him to Bradford, Wigan and Brighton in the space of five months. The first many Pompey fans knew Beasant had finally severed his connections with the club came when he ran out of the tunnel to warm up with the Bradford players when the teams met later in September at Fratton Park. Some thought he was still a Pompey player and had suffered a memory lapse.

and Kawaguchi stuck behind him, there was no room for Beasant and he knew it. Pompey at first wanted him to stay because of his vast experience as the oldest player in the Football League, and because he was still very fit. His greatest moment was undoubtedly the penalty save from Liverpool's John Aldridge in the 1988 FA Cup final while he was an integral part of Wimbledon's Crazy Gang, but

Deon Burton - broken bone in foot put permanent move to Fratton Park in doubt.

"YOU CAN'T WIN 'EM ALL"

Prior to the Gillingham match there was a blow for Pompey when Deon Burton broke a bone in his foot while training and was despatched to Derby to recover, his permanent move in doubt. With Todorov, Pericard and Burchill now available and striking form, Burton went back to Pride Park fearing that it might be the end of his hopes of a fresh start with Pompey. At Priestfield Stadium, Burchill got a starting chance.

Saturday, September 7

GILLINGHAM 1
PORTSMOUTH 3

The Gills are notoriously difficult to beat on their own small ground so Pompey needed to be bold, and they were. Paul Shaw hit the Pompey bar early on before, inevitably, Merson took control. Burchill, justifying his selection, put Taylor away down the left and Merson drove home his centre. Burchill added a second from Todorov's stoppage time pass to give Pompey a solid first-half lead. Gills' substitute Kevin James pulled a goal back in the 68th minute and then missed an open goal. Shaken but not stirred, Pompey came back to claim a third when O'Neil scored off a post. The passer? Merson, of course. Six wins out of seven for Pompey now, and who would have believed that a few weeks ago?

Gillingham (4-4-2): Bartram; Patterson, Ashby, Hope, Edge (Perpetuini 77); Hessenthaler, Smith, Saunders, Shaw; Ipoua, Johnson (James 22).
Subs (not used): Rose, Pennock, Awuah.
Goals: James (68).
Portsmouth (3-4-1-2): Hislop; Primus, Festa, De Zeeuw; Crowe (Harper 63), Hughes, Quashie, Taylor; Merson; Todorov, Burchill (O'Neil 73).
Subs (not used): Kawaguchi, Vincent, Cooper.
Goals: Merson (29), Burchill (45), O'Neil (79).
Attendance: 8,717.
Referee: S Baines (Derbyshire).

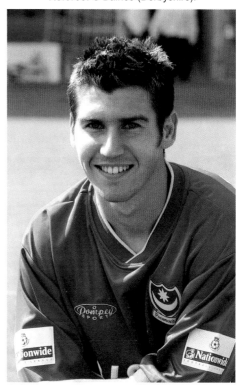

Mark Burchill - justified his selection with an outstanding performance at Gillingham.

Behind the scenes Pompey were still attempting to bring in yet more players, Sherwood discussions were ongoing, hampered by Tottenham's desire for a comparatively small transfer fee, and Fabrizio Ravanelli was always a possibility. Ravanelli, in conflicting reports, appeared keen to join Pompey while his agent was at pains to point out also that he did not want to leave Derby. No other club was in the running for the veteran Italian, whom Jim Smith had ironically taken to Derby from Lazio. Now Derby were thinking of ways of off-loading Ravanelli although he had the best part of a year of his contract remaining. The total cost of that in wages alone was in the region of £2m, money Derby simply could not afford. Pompey offered a way out, suggesting Derby and Pompey shared his wages, but it was an idea that did not appeal to the stricken Midlanders, even in their parlous state. It did not help, either, when Ravanelli returned to Italy to recover from surgery keeping him out of action for several crucial months.

In the circumstances the visit of second division Peterborough in the first round of the Worthington Cup to Fratton Park represented the smallest hurdle of the season so far. But Pompey had been knocked out of the competition at the same stage last season by Colchester and nothing was being taken for granted.

Nigel Quashie - opening goal against Peterborough in the cup.

"YOU CAN'T WIN 'EM ALL"

Tuesday, September 10
Worthington Cup first round

PORTSMOUTH 2
PETERBOROUGH UNITED 0

Peterborough had gone the little matter of 473 minutes without a goal. To that could be added another 90 after Pompey had overcome their spirited challenge. Redknapp's side were never at their best. They did not need to be. Merson was involved in Pompey's opener after 27 minutes, setting up Burchill for a header which was brilliantly parried by impressive keeper Mark Tyler. Nigel Quashie stabbed in the rebound. Barry Fry remonstrated with the referee's assistant after his defender Sagi Burton was sent off for elbowing Todorov, an action unseen by the referee. This took the sting out of Peterborough's determined fightback and it was all over in the 74th minute when Primus finished off good approach play by Todorov. There was a suggestion that Pompey might have rested Merson but the player himself would hear nothing of it.

Portsmouth (3-4-1-2): Hislop; Primus, Festa, De Zeeuw; Crowe (Harper 35), Hughes (Robinson42), Quashie, Taylor; Merson; Todorov, Burchill (Pericard 78).
Subs (not used): Kawaguchi, O'Neil.
Goals: Quashie (27), Primus (74).
Peterborough (5-3-2): Tyler; Pearce, Joseph, Rea, Burton, Newton; Bullard, Danielsson, Shields (Gill 34); Green (A Clarke 45), Fenn (MacDonald 45).

Subs (not used): Lee, Jelleyman.
Booked: Rea.
Sent off: Burton (45).
Attendance: 8,581.
Referee: L Cable (Surrey).

Richard Hughes - failed to last till half-time in the cup match.

The match was not without its drawbacks. Richard Hughes and Jason Crowe failed to reach half time, Crowe limping off in the 35th minute and Hughes, hurt in a collision with Tony Shields, was forced to withdraw seven minutes later. It was the start of more problems for Hughes, who had overcome groin, hernia, hamstring and calf muscle injuries in order to join Pompey. Hughes did not play another league match for six months and when he did, it was for Grimsby on loan.

SLEEPING GIANT AWAKES

Steve Claridge returns to Fratton Park as a Millwall player for the first time since his dismissal as Pompey's boss.

Meanwhile, Burchill's smart return to the first team after such a long absence was not lost on Merson. "Mark looks really sharp," he said. "It's hard to believe that he was injured for so long because he is quick, getting stuck in and looks full of goals. I see no reason why he can't reclaim his place in the Scottish international side." Music to Burchill's ears, no doubt, but he had to be content with a place on the bench for the next match, the eagerly-awaited home clash with Steve Claridge's Millwall.

Portsmouth-born Claridge still lived nearby and remained at heart a Pompey fan. But his summary dismissal after 22 matches as player-manager had hurt him to the core. Claridge wished the club well as a life-long supporter, but there were one or two people within the club to whom he felt less well disposed. Even so, Claridge used the build-up to the game to state his belief that Pompey were geared for promotion. He said: "Harry and Jim have done a great job in a short time. They have brought in some quality players who have mixed together into a decent team. Even at this stage of the season I am convinced they can go up. I hope they do for all their wonderful fans who deserve some success."

"YOU CAN'T WIN 'EM ALL"

Saturday, September 14

PORTSMOUTH 1
MILLWALL 0

Harry Redknapp feared the worst when a head count revealed 12 injured players. But he need not have worried as Pompey recorded their best-ever start to a new season, eclipsing similar efforts in 1922 and 1948. There was a lunchtime kick-off owing to a history of ill-feeling among supporters of both clubs and there was little between the sides. Claridge felt Millwall deserved a draw, Hislop twice denying him and then turning a shot from Christophe Kinet over the bar. Pompey improved with Taylor hitting the bar from 25 yards before Todorov raced clear on to Quashie's defence-splitting pass to lift a shot over the advancing Tony Warner. It wasn't pretty, it wasn't a great performance, but it was three more valuable points.

Portsmouth (3-4-1-2): Hislop; Primus, Festa, De Zeeuw; Harper, Robinson (O'Neil 82), Quashie, Taylor; Merson, Todorov (Tiler 86), Pericard (Burchill 77).
Subs (not used): Kawaguchi, Cooper.
Goals: Todorov (50).
Booked: De Zeeuw, Quashie.
Millwall (4-4-2): Warner; Lawrence (Braniff 85), Nethercott, Ward, Bull; Ifill, Roberts, Livermore, Kinet (Harris 72); Claridge, Davies.
Subs (not used): Gueret, Ryan, Phillips.
Booked: Livermore, Claridge, Davies, Kinet.
Attendance: 17,201.
Referee: S Tomlin (East Sussex).

Todorov lifts his shot over the advancing Tony Warner for Pompey's hard-earned victory over Claridge's Millwall.

Not everything was going Harry Redknapp's way. On the morning of the home league match with Wimbledon he was in court in Southampton facing driving charges. Another speeding fine had got him into trouble and the keys of his top-of-the-range Mercedes were taken from him as magistrates imposed a six-month ban. It's a long way from Portsmouth to Poole when you don't have a car and elder son Mark was pressed into emergency chauffeuring duties. Harry might have struggled to adhere to speeding restrictions but he also makes a bad passenger - as he told an appeal court - and the ban was subsequently reduced, to his relief and that of his driver. A few hours later Pompey were beating Wimbledon, leaving the irrepressible boss to say: "In the morning I got four points and tonight I've got three more."

Tuesday, September 17

PORTSMOUTH 4
WIMBLEDON 1

This was as easy as the score suggests though the Dons could claim that 4-1 was a little harsh. Pompey were ahead in the third minute when Pericard chested down Merson's pass and hooked the ball into the corner of the net. Joel McAnuff, a winger of pace and skill, got down the right to cross for Neil Shipperley to equalise eight minutes later. McAnuff impressed Redknapp so much he even made an inquiry about him, but was scared off by the £2m price tag. Todorov restored Pompey's lead after a typical run down the left but the match was delicately poised until the 39th minute. It was then that goalkeeper Kelvin Davis completely missed a hasty back pass from Mark Williams for the softest of all the goals scored by Pompey in this memorable season. It was not Williams' night. He was later red-carded for a second bookable offence and ten-man Wimbledon were further hit when Taylor scored a blockbuster in the 72nd, collecting a Merson pass on the edge of the area before drilling the ball in off the far post.

Portsmouth (3-4-1-2): Hislop; Primus, Festa, De Zeeuw; Harper (Tiler 88), Robinson, Quashie (O'Neil 86), Taylor; Merson; Pericard, Todorov (Burchill 79).
Subs (not used): Kawaguchi, Vincent.
Goals: Pericard (3), Todorov (31), Williams (OG 39), Taylor (72).
Wimbledon (4-4-2): Davis; Darlington, Williams, Gier (Leigertwood 76), Hawkins; McAnuff, Francis, Andersen, Tapp; Shipperley (Gray 79), Nowland (Ainsworth 86).
Subs (not used): Heald, Willmott.
Goal: Shipperley (11).
Booked: Williams, Tapp.
Sent off: Williams (52).
Attendance: 18,837.
Referee: P Danson (Leicestershire).

Paul Merson, almost disbelieving the pulsating start to the season, issued a 'catch-us-if-you-can' reminder to the rest of the first division as Pompey celebrated their latest success: "We have

"YOU CAN'T WIN 'EM ALL"

Matt Taylor - capped another fine performance
with a blockbuster against Wimbledon.

Scott Hiley - allowed to return to his native Devon after four
years and 75 appearances for Pompey.

shown great quality and togetherness, we are playing some great stuff and long may it continue. If anyone overtakes us between now and the end of the season then they would deserve to be champions."

Meanwhile, Redknapp and Smith were as busy as ever, conscious of the long injury list and anxious to build on the club's early rise to the top. Paul Ritchie, a powerful Scottish left-sided defender, was drafted in on a three-month loan from Manchester City to bolster a squad by now almost picking itself. Redknapp was not so much short of players (there were 35 professionals still on the staff), as short of the quality needed to gain promotion. That is why Ritchie was brought in and Scott Hiley, a former player of the year, was allowed to return to his native Devon to join Exeter, initially on loan. Hiley had not featured in the first team squad so far and although he worked hard in training and was a model professional, he was never going to feature in Redknapp's league team. After almost four years and 75 league appearances, Hiley was on his way.

It had to end sooner or later. Pompey's unbeaten run was almost becoming a millstone in a bizarre sort of way. Norwich, beaten in the play offs, were the team to inflict that first defeat and even then it needed a late goal to finish off Pompey.

Saturday, September 21

NORWICH CITY 1
PORTSMOUTH 0

Norwich were highly fancied at the start of the season after going so close the previous year. When Pompey visited Carrow Road, the Canaries were perched in third place and singing merrily. For about the only time in the whole season Redknapp came under supporter-criticism for picking a defensive formation in which Todorov was the only striker. The aim was to smother Norwich and it so nearly worked. Quashie shaved a post and O'Neil went close and the match had got to the stage, the 81st minute, when both sides were beginning to settle for a draw. Pompey were coming under increasing pressure when that old Welsh gap-toothed warhorse Iwan Roberts got between Festa and De Zeeuw at a corner to score with a typically brave header. "You can't win 'em all," said Redknapp. "I chose the team to do a specific job and it almost paid off. We had the chances to win but it did not happen. We will have learned from this."

Norwich (3-5-2): Green; Kenton, Mackay, Drury; Nedergaard, Emblen (Easton 54), Mulryne, Holt, Heckingbotham; Roberts, McVeigh (Nielsen 88). **Subs (not used);** Crichton, Sutch, Llewellyn. **Goal:** Roberts (81). **Booked:** Holt.
Portsmouth (3-5-1-1): Hislop; Primus, Festa, De Zeeuw; Harper, Robinson (Burchill 83), Quashie, O'Neil (Ritchie 90), Taylor; Merson; Todorov (Pericard 72).

SLEEPING GIANT AWAKES

Paul Merson was finding the hectic schedule of early-season matches a severe test of his fitness and it was after the Norwich match that for the first time he hinted that he might, just might, retire at the end of the season if it also coincided with Pompey reaching the Premiership. It sent shock waves through fans who were becoming accustomed to his silky touch and the number of goals he was making and scoring.

Still there were players coming and going. The latest to leave was Uliano Courville, a French midfield player with a background which included two league appearances for Monaco. Graham Rix brought him to England but he failed to live up to expectations and never appeared in the Pompey first team. Unbelievably, he was the 17th player to go in the six months of the Redknapp reign.

The Ravanelli pot-boiler took another turn when he said: "I would like to join Portsmouth. They are doing well and I like Jim Smith. I feel I can help them win the league." It was getting to the point where the Ravanelli saga was beginning to become dull, but it was to persist for many more months while he recovered from injury.

Saturday, September 28

PORTSMOUTH 3
BRADFORD CITY 0

Would the Norwich defeat signal a downturn in Pompey fortunes? That was the concern of fans as they made their way to Fratton Park for Bradford's visit. They soon got an answer as Pompey bounced back with a vengeance, overwhelming plodding Bradford. The Bantams began brightly enough with Andy Gray and Michael Proctor missing chances but once Nigel Quashie scored from the edge of the area after 17 minutes there was only going to be one winner. Four minutes later Merson put in Pericard for number two and Quashie made sure in the 58th when he ran on to an exquisite pass from Merson for the third. Dave Beasant, on the Bradford bench, could only admire the handiwork of the team he had left. This was a quality display by any standards.

Portsmouth(3-4-1-2): Hislop; Primus, Festa (Ritchie 79), De Zeeuw; Harper, Robinson (O'Neil 71), Quashie, Taylor; Merson; Todorov (Burchill 85), Pericard.
Subs (not used): Kawaguchi, Cooper.
Goals: Quashie(17, 58), Pericard (21).
Bradford (4-4-2): Banks; Uhlenbeek, Molenaar, Bower, Jacobs; Gray, Evans (Reid 64), Jorgensen, Warnock; Cadamarteri (Juanjo 84), Proctor.
Subs (not used): Beasant, Standing, Emanuel.
Attendance: 18,459.
Referee: J Ross (London).

"YOU CAN'T WIN 'EM ALL"

Paul Merson leads the celebrations as Pompey get back to winning ways against Bradford. Despite the constant niggles, his goals and silky passing had been largely responsible for the team riding high at the top of Nationwide League Division One.

So September ended with Pompey still riding high at the top of the first division. Fans had to pinch themselves to make sure they were not dreaming. Opponents, in the main, were not just being beaten but often soundly thrashed. The Norwich defeat was a minor blemish because Pompey were winning - and winning well. Could they keep it up?

TOP 6 AT END OF SEPTEMBER 2002

	P	W	D	L	F	A	Pts
PORTSMOUTH	**11**	**9**	**1**	**1**	**25**	**8**	**28**
Leicester City	11	8	2	1	19	10	26
Norwich City	11	7	3	1	21	7	24
Nottingham Forest	11	6	2	3	22	12	20
Rotherham United	11	5	3	3	20	14	18
Sheffield United	11	5	3	3	15	13	18

6

STONE ROLLS IN

AUTUMN ARRIVED WITH Portsmouth still beaten only once, at Norwich, and the rest of the first division floundering in their wake. Even so, there were still Pompey fans who thought it all a mirage and convinced themselves it could not last. Wait until the heavy grounds arrived, they said.

Harry Redknapp ushered in October by signing Lassina Diabate, an Ivory Coast international from the French club Auxerre. Diabate had extensive experience of top class football in France and in European competition so that his signing was regarded as something of a coup, especially on a free transfer. Diabate said it was his intention to do for Pompey what his friend Ali Benarbia had done for Manchester City the previous season. Benarbia and Diabate were teammates at Bordeaux and Benarbia, late in his career, emerged as the driving force behind City's triumphant return to the Premiership.

And so to the Worthington Cup, that Mickey Mouse competition in which Pompey never seemed to partake beyond the

Lassina Diabate - the Ivory Coast international with a wealth of European experience signed from Auxerre.

early stages. Pompey had failed to get beyond the fifth round in more than 40 years since it first surfaced as the Football League Cup and which had as finalists in its second year that major footballing power, Rochdale.

Tuesday, October 1
Worthington Cup second round

PORTSMOUTH 1
WIMBLEDON 3

After the humiliations at home to second division Colchester the previous year, Pompey had at least seen off Peterborough from the same division in the first round of this year's competition. Having already beaten Wimbledon at home in the league, Pompey were firm favourites to progress to the third round when the teams met again at Fratton Park. Redknapp was still taking the cup seriously and showed his intentions by naming a full-strength team, although Quashie and De Zeeuw were missing with ankle injuries. It was all going according to plan and form when Vincent Pericard finished off a Paul Merson free kick, helped on by Linvoy Primus. Six minutes gone and one up. Right winger Joel McAnuff had been singled out by Redknapp as a danger man and he gave Matt Taylor an uncomfortable evening again. It was McAnuff's shot, a minute later, which struck Taylor and

wrong-footed Hislop for the equaliser. Mikele Leigertwood headed in a corner from Alex Tapp for Wimbledon's second and suddenly the game had been turned on its head. Harper cleared a Leigertwood header off the line before Pompey at last woke up. Taylor had an effort ruled out for offside and Burchill had a couple of penalty appeals rejected. Neil Shipperley rose to head in McAnuff's free kick after 59 minutes and any hopes of a Pompey comeback disappeared when Pericard shot wide of an open goal. Unruffled Redknapp took the loss of Pompey's home

Matt Taylor - an uncomfortable evening at the hands of McAnuff.

record in his stride. He considered the win over Bradford far more important and looked ahead to Saturday's trip to Rotherham. It was, as they say in football, time to concentrate on the league.

> **Portsmouth (3-4-1-2):** Hislop; Primus, Festa, Ritchie; Harper, O'Neil, Robinson, Taylor; Merson; Pericard, Todorov (Burchill 21).
> **Subs (not used):** Kawaguchi, Buxton, Tiler, Cooper.
> **Goal:** Pericard (6).
> **Booked:** Ritchie.
> **Wimbledon (4-4-2):** Davis; Holloway, Leigertwood, Gier, Hawkins; McAnuff, Francis, Andersen, Tapp; Shipperley, Nowland (Gray 67).
> **Subs (not used):** Heald, Willmott, Reo-Coker, Haara.
> **Goals:** McAnuff (7), Leigertwood (16), Shipperley (59).
> **Booked:** Nowland, Hawkins, Tapp.
> **Attendance:** 11,754.
> **Referee:** T Parkes (West Midlands).

For a man considered by Graham Taylor to be on his last legs, Paul Merson was standing up to the rigours of the first division remarkably well. His reputation as a former England player alone meant that in every game he was man-marked and sometimes double-teamed, singled out as Pompey's danger man, but he had already used his knowledge and experience to create a high proportion of his new club's goals as well as getting some important ones of his own. What Taylor must have thought of Merson's well-publicised role in Pompey's rise to the top of the first division has never been known. But while Merson's colossal ability had never been questioned by anyone, his battles

with his many demons had made as many headlines at the peak of his career as had his exploits on the field. Those demons are never far away even now, as he admitted: "The first thing I say when I get up in the morning is 'no drink, no drugs and no bets'. If I didn't, I would be struggling. That's my life." Merson was commuting from his home in St Albans, Hertfordshire, the best part of 100 miles a day, for training at Eastleigh, but so far the transfer to Pompey was giving him a whole new purpose. Better Pompey than Aston Villa's reserves.

Saturday, October 5

ROTHERHAM UNITED 2
PORTSMOUTH 3

The fear that the Wimbledon defeat might spin off into the league again proved unfounded. A trip to Rotherham's cramped Millmoor is never one of the highlights of the season and manager Ronnie Moore, after successive promotions, had made the most of the unprepossessing surroundings and got the best from essentially lower division players. They had responded by lifting Rotherham, almost unnoticed, into fifth position. This was a big test for Pompey and at least they had Quashie and De Zeeuw available again after injury. They needed a good start and got it when Pericard converted Taylor's cross

STONE ROLLS IN

Arjan De Zeeuw - returned to action at Rotherham.

the challenge and Merson duly put away the penalty, bowing theatrically in front of home fans after completing his task. Taylor hit a post with a header as Rotherham struggled to regain their composure only to be thrown a lifeline when referee Laws decided Festa had pulled back substitute Lee. Fleet-footed Lee converted the spot-kick. Reduced to ten men, Rotherham dominated the last 20 minutes and it needed an outstanding save in stoppage time from Hislop to push a 25-yard shot from Paul Hurst on to the bar to prevent an equaliser. The referee was a strong candidate for man of the match, first getting himself noticed when he spotted Hislop was wearing red cycling shorts under his Pompey gear. In his view they were too long and apparently he told Hislop that if he caught sight of them again he would force him to remove them. On or off the pitch, no one quite knew.

at the far post after 15 minutes. Taylor was involved again eight minutes later when his centre was headed down by Pericard for Todorov to claim a second. Rotherham are not so easily overcome and eleven minutes later Darren Byfield nodded in a cross from Chris Swailes. The defining moment of the match came just before half time when Swailes was adjudged to have brought down Todorov in the area. Referee Graham Laws red-carded the luckless Rotherham defender for

Rotherham (4-4-2): Pollitt; Scott, Swailes, McIntosh, Hurst; Sedgwick (Lee 69), Garner, Daws (Monkhouse 85), Warne; Byfield (Mullin 69), Barker.
Subs (not used): Gray, Robins.
Goals: Byfield (34), Lee (pen 73).
Booked: Pollitt, Garner, Byfield, Sedgwick, Scott.
Sent off: Swailes (45).
Portsmouth(4-4-1-1): Hislop; Primus, Festa, De Zeeuw, Ritchie; Pericard, Diabate, Quashie, Taylor; Merson; Todorov (Harper 75).
Subs (not used): Kawaguchi, Robinson, O'Neil, Burchill.
Goals: Pericard (15), Todorov (23), Merson (pen 45).
Booked: Pericard, Quashie, Todorov, Diabate.
Attendance: 8,604.
Referee: G Laws (Tyne and Wear).

SLEEPING GIANT AWAKES

Shaka Hislop - his red cycling shorts caught the attentions of the over-zealous and appropriately named referee, Mr Laws, in the narrow victory at Millmoor.

After the exertions of the early-season, Redknapp gave his players a week off. The match at Wolves, scheduled for Saturday, October 12 was called off because Wolves had three players on international duty. A welcome break for players and management but when Redknapp jetted off for some autumn sunshine and to get away from football, he found Terry Venables, Graeme Souness and Bryan Robson were staying at the same hotel. No prizes for guessing what was discussed around the poolside.

In his absence Carl Robinson was making a small piece of history by being part of the Welsh squad which shocked the football world by beating Italy's aristocrats at the Millennium Stadium, but nearer home the death was announced of Harry Ferrier, the left-back in Pompey's double championship-winning squad of 1948-50. Scotsman Ferrier was described by Pompey legend Jimmy Dickinson as "the finest left-back I ever played in front of" after arriving from Barnsley in August 1946. On occasions when Reg Flewin was absent, he stood in as captain.

Later becoming manager of Chelmsford, he applied for and failed to get the manager's job at Fratton Park when Freddie Cox was fired in 1961.

Another Pompey hero of the past, Peter Harris, one of the few local men in that great side, decided to put his England caps, his championship medals and other football memorabilia up for sale at auction. Now 77, he wanted to buy a car.

Back at troubled Derby, their striker Deon Burton was wondering where his future lay after recovering from an injury sustained training on loan with Pompey. He wanted Pompey to sign himself and Fabrizio Ravanelli, and such was the financial mess at Pride Park, so too did Derby.

As Pompey came back in from their short holiday, it was announced by Exeter that Neil McNab was their new manager. It was not a relationship destined to last long although he quickly returned to Fratton Park to sign Lewis Buxton and Carl Pettefer on loan, Pettefer for the season.

Saturday, October 19

PORTSMOUTH 1
COVENTRY CITY 1

Coventry had been expected to be among the promotion contenders but they were undone by

Above: Harry Ferrier - a member of the double championship-winning side of 1948-50. He died in the week of the win at Rotherham, whilst another member of that side, Peter Harris (below), was forced to sell his medals to buy a car.

Lewis Buxton (above) and Carl Pettefer (below) were to reunite with former Pompey coach Neil McNab at Exeter.

their inconsistency over the season. For Lee Mills, a labouring, injury-prone striker, heavily criticised by fans when he played for Pompey under Tony Pulis, this was a special match. Mills had a premonition of scoring a goal to silence the Fratton hordes but he must have woken at the wrong time. Twice Mills, once Pompey's record signing at £1.2m, struck the woodwork as Coventry played a full part in an entertaining match which could have gone either way. Mills, in top form against his old club, hit the bar from 25 yards just before half-time and then beat Hislop, only to hit a post. None of that stopped him getting his usual round of boos when he was replaced in the 79th minute. Pericard, dreadlocks flowing behind him, put Pompey ahead in the 51st minute, running on to Merson's delicate pass to lob the advancing Babien Dedec. Coventry's equaliser nine minutes later would never win a prize for beauty. Partridge's cross rebounded off two Pompey defenders for Calum Davenport to deflect past Hislop. De Zeeuw headed against the bar, Todorov missed two clear chances and substitute Burchill should have done better from close range. At the other end it needed Hislop's legs to stop Partridge netting a winner. A fair result but, to independent eyes, man of the match honours were contested by Merson and Coventry's 37-year old player-manager Gary McAllister.

STONE ROLLS IN

Portsmouth(4-3-1-2): Hislop; Primus, Festa, De Zeeuw, Taylor; O'Neil (Ritchie 69), Diabate, Quashie; Merson; Todorov (Burchill 84), Pericard.
Subs (not used): Kawaguchi, Harper, Robinson.
Goal: Pericard (51).
Booked: Merson, Diabate.
Coventry (4-5-1): Debec; Caldwell, Davenport, Konjic, Quinn; Pipe (McSheffrey 57), McAllister, Chippo, Safri, Partridge; Mills (Bothroyd 78).
Subs (not used): Hyldgaard, Gordon, Eustace.
Goal: Davenport (60).
Booked: Caldwell.
Attendance: 18,837.
Referee: D Crick (Surrey).

Paul Merson's success at Portsmouth might have helped persuade Steve Stone to join him on the south coast when the former England international midfield player became the latest to experience the coldness of Graham Taylor's shoulder. Stone, his spell at Villa blighted by injuries after a £5m transfer from Nottingham Forest, was getting nowhere under Taylor, ignored for

Todorov battles gamely for the ball against Coventry, but, unusually for him, missed two clear-cut chances. That old warhorse Gary McAllister, the Coventry player-manager, looks on. The 37-year old shared the man-of-the-match honours with Pompey's veteran Merson.

Steve Stone joins the Graham Taylor fan club at Fratton Park and makes an immediate impact.

the Premiership team and costing chairman Doug Ellis a small fortune in wages. Merson it was who recommended Stone to Redknapp, although the Pompey manager was well aware of his Villa Park predicament.

With his usual cunning and spotting a wasted talent, Redknapp arranged for Stone, 31, to spend a month on loan at Fratton Park as the prelude to a full transfer. First he had to be sure that Stone was fit and keen and Stone had to be sure that stepping into the first division, albeit to the club at the top of the table, was the right move. It was another significant signing by Pompey and again they faced no competition, possible competitors frightened off by talk (unsubstantiated) of wages in excess of £20,000 a week. Once more Redknapp hit upon the simple expedient of Pompey paying about half the wages and the rest of the tab being picked up, in this case, by Villa. It was a formula which had stood Redknapp in good stead so far, so that his top wages were still much smaller than those paid by some other clubs in the same division - to the relief of Milan Mandaric, the man with the ultimate responsibility for signing monthly cheques.

The greater turnover in gate receipts and commercial revenue as a result of Pompey's playing success was also welcome after years of major financial losses. Only Mandaric's goodwill and frequent cash injections had saved Pompey from possible extinction in the previous three years and now here was Redknapp bringing in quality players, Merson and Stone (among others), without a cold sweat breaking out on the brow of the club's bank manager.

Not that the spree was over. It never was. Pompey were still in October just about the only club in the top two divisions still actively engaged in recruitment. Football agents, deprived of a buoyant transfer market, fed hungrily on Redknapp's known penchant for buying and selling so that newspaper gossip columns bulged with Pompey links. Burnley's Glen Little and Arthur Gnohere, once a Pompey trialist under Rix, were the latest to be acknowledged by Redknapp as possible targets, while McAnuff and Bristol City's Scott Murray received honourable mentions.

Carl Robinson, still basking in the glory of Italy's defeat by Wales, had done enough to convince the management that after a fitness-proving three-month trial period he should be a given a permanent deal. But no sooner had he put pen to paper on a three-year contract than he started to fall out of the reckoning, and by the New Year Robinson had been allowed to join Sheffield Wednesday and then Walsall on loan, his Pompey career apparently stuttering to a close.

SLEEPING GIANT AWAKES

Saturday, October 26

BURNLEY 0
PORTSMOUTH 3

There were many highlights in a season of high achievement but this win at Burnley's Turf Moor must rank among the best, particularly as Burnley had put together a 12-match unbeaten run. Bald-pated Stone began his Pompey career at right wing-back and later expressed his pleasure at the high standard of his new teammates as they trounced the home side, who were lucky to escape a bigger drubbing. Stone made an impressive start and it was he who released Todorov down the right after 21 minutes. The elusive Bulgarian fooled the Burnley defence, anticipating a cross into the box for Pericard, by finding Quashie to score from the edge. Stone had a goal disallowed for offside and Burnley were glad to get into the dressing room at half time only one behind.

Apoplectic with rage, Stan Ternent's interval 'message' to his Burnley players would not have been kindly. They responded with an improved performance in the second half but Pompey were in no mood to relax their grip. Todorov's mishit shot deceived Beresford in the home goal for the second after 58 minutes and Pompey even survived a

Kevin Harper - the third goal against Burnley.

penalty, harshly awarded when Stone was adjudged to have handled a Briscoe centre. Dean West hit the bar with his spot kick. Taylor cleared off the line for Pompey, whose third goal emanated from the excellent Stone who put Harper away.

There might have been more, Robinson twice going close and Ritchie hitting a post. Wonder what Little and Gnohere made of it?

Burnley (4-3-3): Beresford; West, Cox (Papadopoulos 72), Gnohere, Branch (Maylett 65); Little, S Davis, Briscoe; I Moore (Weller 26), Taylor, Blake. **Subs (not used):** Cook, Grant.

STONE ROLLS IN

Merson immediately implored Redknapp to sign Stone permanently after such a tremendous start. "That was a quality display," he said. "Steve has played for England and spent most of his career at the top level. To get him now would be a real boost because you don't often get players like him for nothing."

While agreeing with Merson's verdict, Redknapp also singled out for praise the much-improved Pericard whose deceptive pace and awkwardness, allied to his non-stop work-rate, had won over sceptical fans. But Pompey's unhappy past had a nasty habit of catching up with them just when it seemed it had all been swept away and forgotten.

Tony Pulis, briefly Pompey's manager, wanted compensation for a large portion of his contract still remaining and the matter got as far as the steps of the High Court before solicitors acting on behalf of the club agreed a way out agreeable to both sides. Pulis, who had also taken Gillingham to court, received around £150,000 from Pompey and three days later he was named as the new manager of first division rivals Stoke. For Mandaric, desperately seeking success to match his colossal input, here was another reminder that it was not to come without a heavy personal cost.

Meanwhile, as the end of the month approached, two long-term crocks, Lee Bradbury and Rory Allen, made welcome returns to action after injury in a reserve team fixture. Allen was

Lee Bradbury returns to action after a ten-month battle with cruciate ligament damage.

back from his eighth operation while the popular former soldier Bradbury was in the process of winning a ten-month battle to overcome cruciate knee ligament damage.

Tuesday, October 29

PORTSMOUTH 3
PRESTON NORTH END 2

Portsmouth fans broke into a spontaneous rendition of "there's only one Graham Taylor" in recognition of his apparent generosity in letting Pompey have Merson and Stone. Did he not like blue and white? Had he been at Fratton Park (and he was not) he would have seen Stone and Merson show class well above first division level as Pompey recorded their seventh home win of the season. Former Scottish international manager Craig Brown had lost only once away all season and in retrospect were by no means the worst side seen at Fratton Park. Brown deployed only one striker, Richard Cresswell, but it was a move which paid off when Hislop could only parry Graham Alexander's shot after 12 minutes for Cresswell to snap up the rebound. On his home debut, Stone was keen to impress and after 23 minutes it was he who finished off Matt Taylor's low centre from close range. It was Pompey's first goal against Preston since 1982.

Steve Stone celebrates his first goal for the club and the club's first goal against Preston since 1982!

Evenly balanced, Pompey got something of a lucky break after 26 minutes when Pericard's stumble on the edge of the area was deemed a penalty and Merson scored his fourth penalty of the season, sending goalkeeper David Lucas the wrong way. The overlapping Taylor got the next, seizing on a deflection to gallop clear before lifting a shot over Lucas as the keeper came out. Cresswell might have narrowed the lead but struck the woodwork instead before Ritchie brought down Mark Rankine to concede the second penalty of the match. Alexander put it away to make it 3-2 and it is fair to say that Preston territorially dominated the rest of an exciting contest. But, committed to attack, Preston almost let in a fourth when substitute Harper struck a post from Merson's cross.

So October ended with Pompey sitting proudly at the top of the first division, as much in control as they had been in August and September. Leicester were now in second place, seven points behind, with the teams due to clash at Fratton Park four days after the Preston match. There was not a cloud in Pompey's sky. But there was some rain on the way.

Portsmouth (3-4-1-2): Hislop; Festa, De Zeeuw, Ritchie; Stone, Diabate, Quashie, Taylor; Merson; Todorov (O'Neil 77), Pericard (Harper 84).
Subs (not used): Kawaguchi, Burchill, Primus.
Goals: Stone (23), Merson (pen 26), Taylor (34).
Booked: Harper.
Preston (3-5-1-1): Lucas; Lucketti, Broomes, Murdock; Alexander, Edwards (Jackson 77), McKenna, Rankine (Etuhu 72), Skora; Lewis (Abbott 68); Cresswell.
Subs (not used): Moilanen, Healy.
Goals: Cresswell (12), Alexander (47).
Booked: Murdock.
Attendance: 18,637.
Referee: P Armstrong (Berkshire).

TOP 6 AT END OF OCTOBER 2002

	P	W	D	L	F	A	Pts
PORTSMOUTH	**15**	**12**	**2**	**1**	**35**	**13**	**38**
Leicester City	15	9	4	2	23	14	31
Norwich City	16	8	6	2	26	11	30
Sheffield United	15	8	4	3	25	18	28
Watford	15	8	3	4	21	21	27
Nottingham Forest	15	7	5	3	26	15	26

7

MONSOON SEASON

THE FORECAST FOR SATURDAY, November 2 was for showers in central southern England, some of them heavy. If that was the case, the heavy ones sought out Fratton Park and deposited their load all over Bob Jones' pride and joy with vindictive pleasure. Portsmouth versus Leicester was already being billed as The Big One, top against second, Harry Redknapp against Micky Adams, a young manager with strong south coast connections and a burgeoning reputation as a man on the up.

A fortnight before Leicester were due at Fratton Park, they had applied to go into financial administration with debts reported to be in the £30m category. Gary Lineker was attempting a rescue package but relegation and the building of the Walkers Stadium had sapped money and morale and key players had been sold to raise funds and ease the wage bill. If some fans thought Pompey were getting above themselves in paying five-figure weekly salaries, they were nothing compared to those at Leicester and, in transfer fees alone, the squad which eventual-ly took the sodden field had cost £15m to assemble. Paul Ritchie, newly-arrived on loan, came up with another forecast of his own, tipping free-flowing Pompey to eclipse Manchester City's 31-win record of the previous season. It was asking a lot of a team still settling in together, but Ritchie was in a good position to make comparisons, and they were favourable.

Saturday, November 2

**PORTSMOUTH 0
LEICESTER CITY 2**

Torrential rain fell in the morning as groundsman Jones and his staff made every effort to drain it from the playing surface, but it had stopped briefly when Birmingham referee Andy Hall made an inspection and, mindful of the occasion and the expected size of the crowd, decided it could go ahead. This was some 90 minutes before the scheduled start and soon afterwards the order was given to open the turnstiles as normal. No sooner had the hapless ref retreated to the sanctuary of his dressing room than the heavens opened again and down it came in bucket-loads so that by the time the players emerged for the pre-match warm-up, the pitch was resembling an extension of the Solent. By this time the crowd, already drenched in some cases, had taken their places and the referee had no option but to at least let the game start. George Best was a guest of the chairman and even he must have struggled to remember an occasion in his own illustrious playing career when he played in such atrocious conditions. Leicester may have lacked a little of Pompey's flair but they were as well organised and methodical as any team put out by Adams and their line up included eight full internationals, not least Muzzy Izzet, a World Cup semi-finalist with Turkey, while million pound men Trevor Benjamin and Andy Impey were on the bench.

This was a big match and everyone was wet even before it started. The referee must have known, as everyone else did, that if it continued to fall in such an unrelenting manner it would not be possible to complete the 90 minutes. Pools of water down the touchlines had players kicking furiously in an increasingly vain attempt to propel the ball forward. Then De Zeeuw and Festa collided so that Festa was unable

George Best shares a joke with Gordana, wife of Milan Mandaric, before the Leicester game. The joke was the state of the pitch.

SLEEPING GIANT AWAKES

**Conditions at Fratton Park for the Leicester game
were nothing short of farcical.**

to continue beyond the half-hour mark, and with Pompey unable to put into operation their fluent pass-and-run game, it was Leicester's more direct approach which was better suited. This was exemplified in the 13th minute when Paul Dickov seized on a long clearance from his goalkeeper to set up James Scowcroft for the opening goal.

The dilemma for the referee was worsening by the minute now that Leicester were ahead. Paul Merson said afterwards that Mr Hall had told him that if Pompey equalised he would call it off. This was never substanti-

ated. Indeed, the referee did not speak to the Press after the match so we shall never know his version of events. The puddles got bigger and bigger and it got even worse for Pompey when Matt Elliott headed in an Izzet corner in the 39th minute. Half time came and it was then that the rain stopped, briefly, but importantly making it all the more difficult for the referee to abandon it, especially as Leicester were two ahead. Ten minutes after the restart, the rain hurled down again and for most of the second half a kaleidoscope of aqua-planing footballers and a stationary ball made for a farcical spectacle. Where play was possible Mark Burchill rounded the keeper only to miss and Quashie and De Zeeuw went close, but Taggart and Elliott were dominant when it mattered and Leicester were comfortable winners.

Festa - knee injury meant he was out until the New Year.

Comfortable was not a word being used by soaked Pompey fans as they made their way into a dismal evening. Not surprisingly the views of the managers differed. Redknapp said: "The game was a nonsense. The conditions were the worst I have ever seen. What you saw out there had nothing to do with football; it was a lottery. I don't know how it started. I told my players to just kick the ball forward, which goes against everything we practise. Merse said the ref had told him when we were one down that he would call it off if we got level. On top of that we have lost Festa with a bad knee injury. But we're still four points clear." Adams said the conditions were not dangerous and were the same for both sides. He also felt his players had been the more eager.

Portsmouth (3-4-1-2): Hislop; Primus, De Zeeuw, Festa (Ritchie 30); Stone, Diabate (O'Neil 54), Quashie, Taylor; Merson; Todorov (Burchill 67), Pericard.
Subs (not used): Kawaguchi, Harper.
Booked: Ritchie, Taylor.
Leicester (4-3-3): Walker; Sinclair, Taggart, Elliott, Davidson; McKinlay, Izzet (Stewart 81), Rogers; Dickov (Benjamin 83), Deane.
Subs (not used): Summerbee, Stevenson, Impey.
Goals: Scowcroft (13), Elliott (39).
Booked: Izzet, Deane.
Attendance: 19,107.
Referee: A Hall (West Midlands).

As Pompey counted the cost of their first home league defeat of the season, they also discovered that the experienced Festa would be out until the New Year with a knee injury, not from colliding with the solidly-built De Zeeuw but from a sliding tackle which took him off the pitch and into a water bottle carrier on the touchline. De Zeeuw sustained a groin injury in the same match and was ruled out for the next at Wolves but the festering resentment felt by Pompey led them to send an official complaint to the Football Association about referee Hall's decision to allow the match to go ahead and be completed. While the FA may have noted Pompey's undisguised fury there was no action taken and the result stood. But the sense of injustice lingered throughout the season, at board level and among supporters, but Leicester noticeably did not join the protests.

Meanwhile, the chairman announced that he was seriously considering offering the frail Best the chance to become an ambassador for the club out of respect for the Irish genius whose every appearance at Fratton Park drew fascinated attention. There was more shuffling of personnel on the training ground as well, Hiley being paid off and signing for Neil McNab's Exeter and the Nigerian international defender Taribo West arriving on trial. Sounded like a fair swap to most Pompey fans; the exotic West, a former Inter Milan star, reuniting with Jim Smith for the first time since they were manager and player at Derby for six months. West was not quite the

player he had been at Pride Park and showed up for his trial some way short of the level of fitness required to perform in the hectic environment of the English first division. Redknapp and Smith both knew that West was a talented footballer who had proved himself at the highest domestic levels in Italy, Germany and England, but even though the trial was extended, no deal was ever agreed due to registration problems and by the end of the month the deeply religious West had gone south to Nigeria. Barry Town later made attempts to sign him, which said something about the state of the transfer market and perhaps about West.

Wednesday, November 6

WOLVES 1
PORTSMOUTH 1

The spectre of Wolves, snatching failure from the jaws of promotion after leading the first division for so long, haunted Pompey throughout the season when they were similarly dominant. The phrase: "We don't want to do a Wolves" was heard among pessimists, expecting Pompey to blow up as Wolves had done the year before in sight of the winning post, surrendering a ten-point lead with ten matches remaining. There was still a sense of Wolves feeling sorry for themselves when Pompey arrived in a bedraggled heap at Molineux with the Leicester debacle still fresh in the memory. The club's coach broke down five minutes after leaving the hotel. Luckily Merson and two directors had their own cars and ferried players to their destination 40 minutes before the kick-off in a manner reminiscent of parks pitch footballers arriving fresh from the pub. Stone played at right-back in a Pompey reshuffle and after Quashie had struck an upright the match exploded when Diabate, who had collected three yellow cards in his first five matches, clattered into George Ndah. To the astonishment of Wolves players and fans, referee Graham Salisbury ruled it a fair challenge and for a time, as Quashie was booked, it all looked as if tempers might boil over. Sanity was restored when Merson put Pompey ahead with a 30-yard free-kick over the defensive wall and beyond Matt Murray. Six minutes later, Dean Sturridge equalised and both sides settled for the draw. Redknapp said: "I would have settled for a point before the game. The first half was like a

Diabate (left) and Quashie (right) made their mark at Molineux in one way or another.

game of chess but the tempo improved in the second. I missed both my first choice centre-halves so it was a makeshift side out there." And what of Diabate? Harry responded: "Diabate would not hurt anyone. He is a pure footballer and if he lacks anything it is aggression." Dave Jones was not so sure: "They are still picking the studs out of George's knee."

Wolves (4-3-3): Murray; Edworthy, Lescott, Clyde, Irwin; Ince, Rae, Cooper (Newton 82); Blake (Sturridge 15), Ndah (Kennedy 34), Miller.
Subs (not used): Oakes, Ingimarsson.
Goal: Sturridge (62).
Booked: Sturridge, Ince.
Portsmouth(4-4-2): Hislop; Stone, Primus, Ritchie, Taylor; Diabate (O'Neil 76), Quashie, Robinson (Harper 52), Merson; Todorov (Burchill 71), Pericard.
Subs (not used): Kawaguchi, Cooper.
Goal: Merson (56).
Booked: Stone, Robinson, Quashie.
Attendance: 27,022.
Referee: G Salisbury (Lancashire).

Finnish international Markus Heikkinen was a new name to be linked with Pompey, a footballing centre half at HJK Helsinki, whom Redknapp eventually signed on a three month trial in January with a view to the future rather than the present, but the restless determination of the manager to keep building an entirely new staff showed he was not completely satisfied with the squad he possessed.

There was good news for Todorov who had been as mysteriously under-used by his country as he had been by West Ham.

But his return to goalscoring form with Pompey, reinvigorated by the fresh challenge, earned him a recall to the Bulgarian squad for the friendly with Spain later in November. It was a tribute to Todorov's determination to get back into the national team and a tribute to Redknapp for spotting and developing a player not wanted elsewhere.

Todorov - a recall to his national side for the friendly with Spain was a tribute to both himself and Redknapp.

MONSOON SEASON

Saturday, November 9

DERBY COUNTY 1
PORTSMOUTH 2

Deon Burton and Fabrizio Ravanelli had been so much a part of the Pompey story so far that an outsider could have been led into believing they were actually Pompey players. Burton had spent a spell on loan and kept saying he wanted a permanent move while Ravanelli made it clear he was just as keen to follow Burton to Fratton Park. So it was almost a surprise to see them both on the Derby bench when Pompey headed for Pride Park.

For Jim Smith it was a nostalgic trip back to the club he had managed and he received a warm welcome. No one was blaming him for the financial mess. Derby were now, of course, in the hands of ex-Pompey boss John Gregory, a man who on becoming manager at Fratton Park - his first senior post - boasted that on his desk were pictures of his mentors, Terry Venables and Arthur Cox, to act as spiritual spurs and inspirational guides. Gregory was cheering with delight when Danny Higginbotham scored from the penalty spot after Lee Morris had been brought down by Diabate. But Pompey's goalscoring power, a potent weapon when all other areas

Jim Smith - nostalgic return to Pride Park.

were equal, was evident again when Todorov put away their first serious chance from Taylor's cross. Foxe appeared as a second-half substitute after one training session in ten weeks in place of Ritchie. Pompey's winner came five minutes after half-time when Merson and Taylor were at the hub of a move, as they were so often throughout the season, which led to Burchill scoring. Burton and Ravanelli came on as late subs in an effort

Hayden Foxe - a return to action after a ten week lay-off.

to save the match but the Pompey defence held firm, as it always did.

At the final whistle Redknapp emerged from his dug-out to punch the air with delight while saluting the 4,000 travelling fans. He said: "The win at Burnley was great but beating Derby was better. They have got more strength in depth than us with Burton and Ravanelli on the bench. I thought we were terrific in the second half. We played some great stuff after going a goal behind and if it hadn't been for the ref we might have got more. They didn't give us the most obvious penalty you have ever seen. Merse has got a big gash down the back of his Achilles where Rob Lee caught him. It's a great result for Jim Smith." As for Gregory, where were those pictures of Venables and Cox when he needed them?

Derby (3-4-1-2): Grant; Higginbotham, Evatt (Ravanelli 70), Barton; Boertien, Bolder, Lee, Hunt (Riggott 16); Kinkladze; McLeod (Burton 82), Morris.
Subs (not used): Oakes, Twigg.
Goal: Higginbotham (pen 16).
Booked: Kinkladze, Boertien.
Portsmouth (3-4-1-2): Hislop; Primus, De Zeeuw, Ritchie (Foxe 45); Stone, Diabate, Quashie, Taylor; Merson; Todorov (Harper 89), Burchill (Pericard 81).
Subs (not used): Kawaguchi, Robinson.
Goals: Todorov (27), Burchill (51).
Booked: Diabate, Quashie, Todorov.
Attendance: 26,587.
Referee: H Webb (South Yorkshire).

And now, the Strange Case of Rory Allen. Every butcher, baker and candlestick-maker has dreamt of handing in his notice to try his hand at something less humdrum. But it is rare, indeed exceptional, for a pampered footballer on four-figure wages every week to wish to do the same. Rory Allen did. Fed up with constant injuries and eight operations, the former Spurs player could see no future either at Fratton Park, where the competition for striking places was now intense, or at any other club. Not having played in the Pompey first team for two-and-a-half years, Allen's career reached rock-bottom in a reserve match at Plymouth on a deserted university pitch and against eager teenagers. Some time around then he must have decided that he no longer wanted to be a professional footballer. So with money in his pocket, Allen simply decided to quit, informing Pompey that he was off to join that travelling band of cricket-supporters, the Barmy Army, for the Ashes tour of Australia. Pompey first discovered Allen's desire for some winter sunshine when he failed to show up for training. Peter Storrie vowed to study tapes of the Barmy Army to see if he could spot Allen waving a patriotic flag while knocking back a cold lager. "There are some release forms for him to sign," he said. Rory Allen never was picked out of the crowd and no one knew what happened to him. Football lost a talented footballer and cricket gained an avid new fan. Whether he would have played any part in Pompey's promotion season or not is immaterial but the manager would certainly have played him in the first match had he not been injured yet again.

Rory Allen - the injury-prone striker decided the England cricket team's needs were greater and joined the Barmy Army in Australia.

Saturday, November 16

PORTSMOUTH 3
STOKE CITY 0

This was a match which brought Tony Pulis back to Fratton Park for the first time since his sacking by Pompey, giving him the chance to pit his wits against Redknapp. They were old friends, Redknapp rescuing Pulis's playing career at Bournemouth after Newport County had freed him and later Pulis becoming coach at Dean Court before succeeding Redknapp as manager. It is fair to say that the respective footballing philosophies of Pulis and Redknapp were not similar, but there was a mutual respect and Redknapp went on record to say he believed Pulis was the man to stop Stoke going straight back into the second division. Stoke bore all the Pulis trademarks of hard work and competitiveness even after only two weeks in charge. Pompey found it difficult to break down opposition which played with Tommy Mooney as its sole striker and packed the midfield. Switching to 4-4-2 for the second half, Pompey at last got on top and once Burchill had converted Harper's low cross at the near post in the 49th minute there was only going to be one winner. Even so Pompey had to wait until the last three minutes before scoring two more through

MONSOON SEASON

Pulis returns to Fratton Park with Stoke City.

Pericard and Todorov. Redknapp admitted: "We are not always going to play well. They made it hard for us by playing five across the middle and one up front. Lots of teams are doing that at Fratton Park to stop us playing but we always seem to wear them down."

Portsmouth (3-4-1-2): Hislop; Primus, Foxe, De Zeeuw; Harper (Crowe 88), Diabate, Quashie, Taylor; Merson; Todorov (O'Neil 90), Burchill (Pericard 66).
Subs (not used): Kawaguchi, Robinson.
Goals: Burchill (49), Pericard (87), Todorov (90).
Booked: De Zeeuw.
Stoke (4-5-1): Cutler; Henry, Thomas, Handyside, Clarke; Gudjonsson (Iwelumo 84), Gunnarsson, Marteinsson (Greenacre 84), O'Connor, Hoekstra (Vandeurzen 84); Mooney.
Subs (not used): Viander, Cooke.

Booked: Clarke, Marteinsson.
Attendance: 18,701.
Referee: P Taylor (Herts).

Steve Stone was sent back to Villa for treatment on a hamstring injury and, in his absence, Redknapp asked the chairman for more money for more players. So far Mandaric had responded, digging deep when it mattered to maintain Pompey's position at the top of the table and as the number one club in the country for transfer activity. Gordon Strachan, manager of Southampton, was already looking forward to possible derby matches and congratulated Pompey on such a fine start to the season. Strachan said: "Milan Mandaric's financial backing has been such that Pompey fans should get down on their hands and knees and give thanks. I cannot think of many grounds more intimidating than Fratton Park." Redknapp, meanwhile, feared that Fratton Park, with its limited capacity, would impede Pompey's progress should they ever go up.

Saturday, November 23

SHEFFIELD WEDNESDAY 1 PORTSMOUTH 3

Pompey had traditionally failed in front of Sky TV cameras in the past and fears doubled when star man Merson limped off half way through the first half with an injured ankle, Craig Armstrong somehow escaping a caution after a horrendous lunge at the Pompey skipper. But there was no need to worry. Pompey saw off the television jinx and managed perfectly well without Merson. It certainly helped that Wednesday were abject opposition. Todorov, shrugging off a virus which forced him to miss his international recall, put Pompey ahead but Leon Knight equalised soon after Merson had limped off. Gary O'Neil slotted into Merson's position and gave a polished performance for a 19-year old. Todorov struck again after the break and O'Neil showed signs of coming of age with the third after 64 minutes. Wednesday had no answer. But there were problems. Primus departed with a groin injury and Diabate's fifth booking guaranteed him a rapid-time ban. Redknapp was unmoved: "Seven away wins is unbelievable. We keep coming away with results at places where Portsmouth have struggled for years. Toddy was outstanding again and Pericard has done better than I ever expected. I don't think their player went out to hurt Merson. It was the same with Diabate at Wolves. That's football."

Sheffield Wednesday (3-4-1-2): Pressman; Crane, Haslam, Bromby; Geary, Quinn, Armstrong, Beswetherick (Hamshaw 76); Sibon; Knight, Owusu (Donnelly 76).
Subs (not used): Stringer, Hendon, Morrison.
Goal: Knight (27).
Booked: Beswetherick.

Portsmouth (3-4-1-2): Hislop; Primus (Crowe 60), Foxe, De Zeeuw; Harper, Diabate, Robinson, Taylor; Merson (O'Neil 24); Todorov (Burchill 80), Pericard.
Subs (not used): Kawaguchi, Pitt.
Goals: Todorov (11, 50), O'Neil (64).
Booked: Diabate, De Zeeuw.
Attendance: 16,602.
Referee: P Danson (Leicester).

Redknapp might have been prepared to forgive Armstrong for his tackle on Merson, but Merson was not. As he went away for a scan to find the extent of the injury which was to bother him for some weeks, he said: "If he had followed through, rather than hit my ankle, he would have broken my leg. I'm surprised it has taken 21 games for someone to try to kick me."

Meanwhile, the season had reached the stage where mind games were starting to be played. Micky Adams, his team beaten by Preston, said the title was Pompey's but Redknapp saw through it: "He's dreaming. We are not even half way through the season." Instead, Redknapp revealed that taking Pompey into the Premiership would be the pinnacle of his 20-year managerial career at the same time as making inquiries (rebuffed) for Blackburn's Andy Todd and John Curtis. Then, on the eve of the home match with Walsall, Merson, after narrowly passing a fitness test on his sore and swollen foot, muttered about retirement at the end of the season. It was not the ideal prelude.

Gary O'Neil - slotted perfectly into the injured Merson's position against Sheffield Wednesday and responded with a polished performance.

Redknapp - reacted to Merson's ankle injury at Hillsborough with calmness. "That's football," he said. Merson, however, was not so forgiving.

Saturday, November 30

**PORTSMOUTH 3
WALSALL 2**

Managers are never happy until they reach the magical 50 points mark because it usually means survival has been achieved. In three of the previous five seasons Pompey had stayed up without even getting 50 points so it was a measure of the club's progress under Redknapp and Smith that the target was hit on the last Saturday of November. The crowd even sang: "We're staying up" at the final whistle in mock celebration. Walsall went away feeling they should have at least drawn but Pompey's superior firepower enabled them to overcome a horrendous injury list which forced Merson and Foxe into playing despite not training in the week. De Zeeuw was suspended while Primus, Festa and Stone joined the long-term absentees. At least Quashie was available again after suspension and Ritchie made a swift recovery from torn stomach muscles.

Walsall were full of menace early on with Brazilian Junior hitting the bar and Danny Sonner opening the scoring with a penalty after Ritchie had fouled Steve Corica. It was not until first-half stoppage time that Quashie equalised and then in the second half revitalised Pompey scored through a Todorov header from Merson's corner. Jason Crowe then fouled Sonner to give the same player a penalty he put away with relish to set up a fascinating finish. A 16-man ruck went unpunished by referee Grant Hegley and Redknapp was banished to the stands after clashing heatedly with the fourth official. With 14 minutes remaining Sonner lost possession and, after Quashie and Pericard had efforts blocked, Taylor ran in the winner. There was still time for Hislop to deny

Todorov glides through the Walsall defence to put Pompey 2-1 in front, his fifth goal in four matches in November.

substitute Gary Birch an equaliser before Mr Hegley blew for full-time while standing near the touchline. As the first man off the pitch, he made a quick exit to the safety of his dressing room, avoiding the wrath of both managers, both sets of players and both sets of supporters.

Portsmouth (3-4-1-2): Hislop; Crowe, Foxe, Ritchie; Harper, Diabate, Quashie, Taylor; Merson (Burchill 89); Todorov (Buxton 90), Pericard (O'Neil 85).
Subs (not used): Kawaguchi, Robinson.
Goals: Quashie (45), Todorov (58), Taylor (76).
Booked: Ritchie, Quashie, Taylor.
Walsall (3-4-1-2): Walker; Pollet, Hay, Roper; Bazeley, Sonner, O'Connor, Wrack; Corica; Junior (Birch 64), Leitao.
Subs (not used): Ward, Aranalde, Carbon, Simpson.
Goals: Sonner (31, 68 pens).
Booked: Sonner, Wrack, Leitao.
Attendance: 17,701.
Referee: G Hegley (Herts).

TOP 6 AT END OF NOVEMBER 2002

	P	W	D	L	F	A	Pts
PORTSMOUTH	**21**	**16**	**3**	**2**	**47**	**20**	**51**
Leicester City	21	13	5	3	33	20	44
Nottingham Forest	21	11	6	4	38	20	39
Norwich City	21	11	6	4	34	17	39
Reading	20	12	2	6	24	14	38
Sheffield United	20	10	5	5	33	24	35

Matt Taylor, the scorer of Pompey's winner, typifies the team's determination.

8

DOING A WOLVES

DECEMBER WAS THE ONLY month in which Pompey did not carry all before them in the way they had done in the previous four months. One win and four draws represented more of a wobble than a crisis. The victory at Nottingham Forest on the 28th went a long way to convincing worried fans that there was nothing terminal about Pompey's slight decline from their own high standards.

The month began with the usual plethora of transfer links and a warning from chairman Mandaric that this season, however successful, might be his last in the hot seat. The new name to emerge as a genuine target was Les Ferdinand who, in his Queen's Park Rangers and New-castle heyday, had won 17 England caps but who at 36 was now no more than a fringe play-er at Glenn Hoddle's Tottenham. Mandaric had made it clear that there was still money left for recruitment and Ferdinand felt he still had a year or two to offer. It was ironic that Redknapp's former club, West Ham, were as keen on signing him and both clubs took the opportunity to open negotiations once Hoddle had made it clear that Ferdinand was not part of his plans. Even being linked with someone of Ferdinand's calibre was an indi-cation of how far Pompey had developed in the last nine months. Who would have thought back in March, in the dark days of Rix's departure, that Pompey would sign players like Merson and Stone and be chasing a player like Ferdinand?

This was not lost on the Portsmouth public and the club were able to announce that sea-son tickets had hit the 15,000 mark for the first time. But that news was tempered by Man-daric's evident indecision about his future. Three and a half years bankrolling Pompey had taken a toll on his finances. The lure of a retirement to the Californian sunshine and family life uninter-rupted by frequent trips to the grey of wintering England to sign cheques was proving stronger by the day. In an interview with Mark Storey, chief football writer of The News, Portsmouth, he said: "If we go up I can look everyone in the eye and say I ful-filled what I promised to do when

SLEEPING GIANT AWAKES

**Milan Mandaric - his statement that he may leave
the club at the end of the season sent shockwaves
through the Pompey public.**

I came here. Then I'm free; then I can go away. That's very possible. If I decide to go, I'm free to go. If I decide to stay it will require another three-year commitment. I will make up my mind in April." Chief executive Peter Storrie, mindful of the loss to the club if Mandaric carried out his threat, refused to believe that the chairman would relinquish his grip once promotion had been achieved. He said: "If Milan is enjoying himself now, being top of the first division, he'll love it in the Premiership. It is a different world." Fans in the Ty Europe Stand, the old Fratton End, aware of what Mandaric had done for their club, redoubled their favourite chant of "Milan, there's only one Milan", hoping to appeal to his sentimental side and to show how much he was wanted. But there was just a hint of desperation about the rendition in the matches following his public searching of the soul.

Disappointingly, Ferdinand opted for West Ham and the new target, Sheffield Wednesday's Shefki Kuqi, with no disrespect, did not appear to fans to be in the same league. Meanwhile, the squad assembled by Ball/Pulis/Claridge/Rix was still in evidence and Neil Barrett, a midfield player who had made a favourable impression among supporters in his first season with Pompey but who was out of favour under Redknapp, head-

ed for Notts County on trial. Later in the month, Tom Curtis, a £150,000 signing by Pulis from Chesterfield in August 2000, was shipped off to Mansfield for nothing, his seven starts costing the club in excess of £20,000 each plus, of course, the obligatory pay-off.

And so to Reading's 24,000 capacity Madejski Stadium. Reading had come a long way since John Madejski had done for his home-town club what Mandaric was doing for Pompey. Historically, Reading had not

Left: Neil Barrett, out of favour under Redknapp, headed for Notts County and, above, Tom Curtis, just seven starts for Pompey costing some £20,000 each, went to Mansfield.

Pompey's number one fan - antiquarian bookseller John Westwood was forced to miss his first match since 1996 when refused admission at Reading.

been a big club and had matched modest ambitions with limited, lower division achievements. But with a superb new stadium and with money spent on putting together a powerful second division team, they had raced through the first to become unexpected promotion rivals. It was one of Pompey's derby matches and some 4,500 Pompey fans travelled over the border to Berkshire for a lunchtime kick-off. Shaka Hislop shrugged off flu to keep his ever-present record.

Saturday, December 7

READING 0
PORTSMOUTH 0

Keeping an ever-present record was something which sadly eluded John Westwood, Pompey's number one fan, who had changed his name by deed poll to John Portsmouth Football Club Westwood to honour the club he loved. Wearing his legendary long blue wig underneath a blue and white top hat and with a bugle always at hand, he had watched every match home and away played by Pompey since 1996, his outlandish appearance at variance with his day-time job as an antiquarian bookseller in genteel Petersfield. Having purchased a ticket in advance, Westwood, who had been voted supporter of the year by the admiring Mandaric the previous

season, was refused entry at the turnstiles without reason, leaving him outside to gauge the balance of the match from crowd noises within, squinting through gaps in closed turnstile doors for glimpses of a game he had been forbidden to see.

What Westwood missed was an exciting battle in which Pompey were happy to escape with a draw. Reading had won their previous six matches without conceding a goal and were now in fifth place, 13 points behind the leaders. Matthew Upson, on loan from Arsenal, had been a major reason why Reading's defence had been so secure, and in the knowledge that he was returning to Arsenal's reserves, Redknapp immediately expressed an interest in signing him. Later Upson chose Birmingham. Diabate was suspended and two former Royals, Linvoy Primus and Hislop, faced their old club. Hislop it was who ensured a point with a brilliant double save from Nicky Forster and John Salako. The Burchill-Todorov partnership failed to work up front and it was not until five minutes from time that Pompey forced their first corner. Home keeper Marcus Hahnemann did not have a save to make.

Redknapp said: "It was a good point away from home. They are a very, very good side and I can see how they have gone so long without conceding a goal. We had a lot of possession without hurting them. But I only had 12 players training all week. Paul Merson did not train at all and needed an injection in his foot to be able to play."

Reading (4-4-1-1): Hahnemann; Murty, Williams, Upson, Shorey; Rougier (Butler 79), Harper, Newman (Watson 64), Salako; Hughes (Cureton 71), Forster.
Subs (not used): Ashdown, Tyson.
Portsmouth (4-3-1-2): Hislop; Primus, De Zeeuw, Foxe, Ritchie; Robinson, Quashie, Taylor; Merson; Todorov, Burchill (Harper 45).
Subs (not used): Kawaguchi, O'Neil, Crowe, Pitt.
Booked: Quashie.
Attendance: 23,462.
Referee: A Leake (Lancashire).

The draw for the third round of the FA Cup is always eagerly awaited and on the day after the Reading match Pompey got lucky in a big way. Every smaller club wants Arsenal or Manchester United and, to a roar of delight which must have reverberated around the city, Pompey were drawn away to Manchester United. Mandaric misheard the excited tones of the radio announcer and thought his club had been drawn to play at third division Macclesfield. Only when Redknapp called him on his mobile did he realise his mistake. Cup fever quickly gripped Portsmouth and even when Sky TV announced that the match would be televised, it failed to dampen the massive enthusiasm for tickets. Television money alone guaranteed Pompey £1m and, when 9,000 tickets went on sale to season ticket holders, queues formed

Shaka Hislop - in superb form against his former club despite suffering from 'flu.

overnight and continued to grow even as rain made their vigil miserable and uncomfortable. Men, trapped at work, sent wives and girlfriends to huddle under umbrellas until such time as they were able to take their place in the wet snake which wound its way down Frogmore Road and beyond. Guy Walton was typical. He had made a 200-mile trip to ensure that he could take his seat at the Theatre of Dreams. Such is the magic of the FA Cup. Mandaric, impressed at the profit his club would be making, invited United legend George Best to be his guest at Old Trafford.

Redknapp, meanwhile, was not taking his eye off immediate requirements and, after protracted negotiations, was able to secure the permanent signing of Deon Burton. Eventually it was agreed that Derby would receive around £200,000 if Pompey went up, small beer for a player with extensive Premiership experience and still to reach his peak. Burton, anxious to escape the monetary chaos at Pride Park, said: "I was at a club going in the wrong direction and I have joined one going in the right direction. My job now is to help the club get into the Premiership. I am sure we will get there." Pompey told the world that Yoshi was available (again) and it became clear also that Steve Stone would be the next signing.

Saturday, December 14

STOKE CITY 1
PORTSMOUTH 1

Tony Pulis was still searching for his first win as Stoke manager and was keen to prevent Pompey becoming the sixth club in succession to win at the Britannia Stadium. For Burton, it was a return to familiar territory. Only last May, while on loan from Derby, the Jamaican international had ensured promotion from the second division for Stoke by scoring in the play-off final against Brentford at the

Deon Burton - signs on a permanent basis from Derby.

Millennium Stadium. Pompey were without the suspended Taylor and his powerful runs forward were missed as Stoke took the lead when Wayne Thomas's cross was headed back by Sergei Shtaniuk for Brynjar Gunnarsson. Only a last-ditch tackle by Diabate stopped Chris Greenacre adding a second in a disappointing first half display from Pompey.

Redknapp switched to a more progressive formation for the second half, with Crowe and Harper coming on to play as wing-backs. It worked. Pompey were much better after the break and, after mounting pressure, Crowe scored from a yard to earn a draw. Redknapp was generous in his praise for Pulis: "Stoke's first half performance was as good as any team have produced against us. Tony Pulis will do a good job for them. We seem to be a bit of a second half team at the moment but we can't afford to be like that. We were satisfied with a point. The team looked to be more comfortable playing in a wing-back formation." Pulis was equally happy to praise the team put out by his old friend. Only Quashie, Primus and Harper remained of his own signings as Pompey manager, such had been the turnover of players in the two years since he departed Fratton Park. Pulis said: "Pompey are the best passing side in the division so I was pleased that in the first half we played the best since I have been at Stoke. In the second half Pompey were terrific and the match was a great advert for the first division."

Stoke (4-4-2): Banks; Thomas, Shtaniuk, Handyside, Hall; Gudjonsson, Gunnarsson, Henry (Goodfellow 79), Neal (Marteinsson 63); Cooke, Greenacre (Mooney 79).
Subs (not used): Cutler, Iwelumo.
Goal: Gunnarsson (34).
Booked: Henry, Shtanuk, Gunnarsson.
Portsmouth (4-3-1-2): Hislop; Primus, De Zeeuw, Foxe, Ritchie (Harper 45); Robinson (Crowe 74), Diabate, Quashie; Merson; Todorov, Burton.
Subs (not used): Kawaguchi, O'Neil, Burchill.
Goal: Crowe (74).
Booked: Crowe, Diabate.
Attendance: 13,300.
Referee: P Walton (Northamptonshire).

Matt Taylor's stunning introduction to the first division after playing for Luton in the third had inevitably led to Premiership clubs wondering why they had not also spotted the raw talent lingering in the lower divisions. Recruiting more and more from abroad, Premiership clubs had got out of the habit at looking for uncut diamonds on their own doorstep. In contrast, Redknapp had never forgotten his formative managerial years at Bournemouth, scouring for players at near-deserted non-league grounds or driving home through the night after watching a reserve match up country. Efan Ekoku and Shaun Teale were signed by him for Bournemouth from non-league clubs and went on play in the top flight. Taylor was a typical Redknapp signing to those who knew how he worked, nipping in where rivals dithered, backing his judgement on knowing a good player when he saw one. Now Taylor was attracting attention, allegedly from Chelsea. "Hands off," Redknapp said. "We have no intention of selling our best players." One player not coming to Pompey was the Finnish striker Kuqi, who had been playing well in a poor Sheffield Wednesday side. Redknapp liked the look of him, but not of his wage demands: "I have spoken to his agent and he's talking silly money. He's in cloud cuckoo land." Perhaps he meant cloud-Kuqi land.

While Kuqi slipped the net, Steve Stone was only too keen to be enmeshed in it. A few days

Matt Taylor - a typical Redknapp signing and now coveted by Premiership clubs.

Steve Stone - signs on the dotted line for Pompey in another of Redknapp's familiar deals.

before Christmas, Aston Villa's former England player readily agreed to follow former team-mate Paul Merson to Fratton Park on a free transfer. It was a deal familiar to many hatched by Redknapp whereby Villa paid him off allowing Pompey to negotiate more reasonable wages, around half of what he had been receiving at Villa Park. Stone was not as withering in his condemnation of Graham Taylor as Merson had been, but there was hurt when he said: "I am still keen to show that I can play in the Premiership. I don't think I was given a fair chance at Villa but I would not have signed for Pompey if I did not think they would be playing in the Premiership next season."

Saturday, December 21

PORTSMOUTH 1
IPSWICH TOWN 1

Ipswich came to Fratton Park in a state of some disarray. They were finding the financial burdens of relegation insurmountable. Top players had already been sacrificed and others were to follow as the club, once an admired model of prudence, drifted into administration. George Burley, a true son of Ipswich football, had been fired and when the Tractor Boys hit Portsmouth they were under new management and well adrift in the lower half of a table they had been expected to dominate. Joe Royle had managed to steady the ship but in terms of points and positions they were well adrift of Pompey before the kick-off on that foggy pre-Christmas Saturday. When the match was over it was clearer why Ipswich had been pre-season favourites to go straight back up. They had the

Todorov puts Pompey ahead after a mistake by Ipswich goalkeeper Andy Marshall.

better of an exciting match, best remembered for a trio of terrible misses in front of goal by Ipswich's striker Pablo Counago. It was Pompey who went ahead, Andy Marshall spilling a cross from Taylor into the path of Todorov. Richard Naylor hit the Pompey bar before defender Thomas Gaardsoe headed in an equaliser from a corner. Ipswich had Chris Makin sent off for fouling substitute Burchill and, as Pompey went in search of a winner, Marshall atoned for his mistake with a great save from Burchill's header.

Redknapp, sensing some disquiet, pointed out that Pompey's last three fixtures had not been easy, nor had he expected them to be: "Reading had not dropped a point for a long, long time. Stoke is not an easy place to go and Ipswich are a very good side. I expected them and Leicester to be the best two sides in the division and fighting for the championship." Redknapp also mystified some sections of the Fratton faithful when he took off Merson, for whom a foot injury was showing no signs of improvement. He explained: "I took Paul off because we were outnumbered in midfield. He had injections before the game and at half-time. Step back and look at the big picture. We are 12 points clear of Forest in third place. We have got to be pleased with that." As for Royle, he said: "We were disappointed not to have won it

because we had the better chances. Harry said we were the best side they had played all season."

Portsmouth (3-4-1-2): Hislop; Primus, Foxe, De Zeeuw; Stone (Harper 88), Diabate, Quashie, Taylor; Merson (O'Neil 73); Todorov, Burton (Burchill 85).
Subs (not used): Kawaguchi, Ritchie.
Goal: Todorov (19).
Booked: Diabate, Foxe, Taylor.
Ipswich (3-5-2): Marshall; Holland, Gaardsoe, Makin; Wilnis, T Miller, Clapham, Magilton (Wright 83), Hreidarsson; Counago (D Bent 80), Naylor (M Bent 59).
Subs (not used): Pullen, Ambrose.
Goal: Gaardsoe (54).
Booked: T Miller, Hreidarsson, Makin.
Sent off: Makin (90).
Attendance: 19,130.
Referee: G Barber (Hertfordshire).

Lee Bradbury was a butt for crowd fury at Manchester City where fans unkindly referred to him as Lee Badbuy after two indifferent years (ten goals in 40 league appearances). It was not his fault that the fee changing hands was £3.5m but in two spells at Portsmouth either side of that at Maine Road they had seen the best of his tenacity, bravery, hard work and sharpness in front of goal. But before Redknapp had taken over, Bradbury suffered the injury all footballers fear, cruciate knee ligament damage. It invariably requires an operation and many players are never the same again on their return. Now Isle of Wight-born Bradbury was on the mend and in need of games to accelerate his recovery. It was at this point that Sheffield Wed-

Lee Bradbury: A catalogue of injuries and bad luck.

nesday's new manager Chris Turner decided to take him on loan, something of a gamble as Bradbury, for all his willingness, had not played at this level for ten months. It was typical of Bradbury's wretched luck that

within a few weeks he was on the operating table again, this time to cure a shoulder injury, his comeback delayed yet again. As consolation, Redknapp made it clear that he had time for Bradbury and it was obvious he did not regard him with the disdain in which he held many of the others he had inherited. Luke Nightingale, another of the forgotten army still on the payroll, headed to Swindon on a trial which was allied to the need to regain fitness after long-term knee trouble. It did not work out. He made only two starts and was packed off back to Fratton Park and Pompey reserves by Swindon manager Andy King as soon as his loan expired.

Thursday, December 26

PORTSMOUTH 1
CRYSTAL PALACE 1

Pompey trained on Christmas Eve and had a lighter session on Christmas Day before the difficult match with unpredictable Palace. Palace had a reputation as draw specialists and this was their tenth. For Pompey it was their fourth in succession and there was a suggestion of anxiety about their performance when Palace showed they were no pushovers. Merson was clearly not fit but he still raced half the length of the pitch to turn in a low centre from Taylor at the far post to give Pompey the lead. Todorov hit the bar and Merson went close again in a bright spell but within three minutes of the goal, Palace were level when Julian Gray crashed in an equaliser from Danny Butterfield's right-wing cross. O'Neil hit the bar for Pompey but it needed another class piece of keeping from Shaka Hislop to prevent Ade Akinbiyi getting a late Palace winner. There were boos at the final whistle, not an uncommon sound in previous years, but a surprise to those who had watched some exhilarating football this year. They had hardly been warranted and even after dropping two points, Pompey were still ten clear of Sheffield United in third place.

Harry Redknapp went on the offensive in his post-match press conference when a hapless hack from a popular newspaper suggested Pompey were on the blink. He snapped: "Yes, you're right. The wheels have come off. I think we could be in for a relegation battle. It's very similar to Wolves. We've lost two games all season. It's been terrible. Pompey fans have got used to a winning team over the last few years, haven't they? What a stupid question. I don't know." With that he was gone, turning tail and heading off into the night, home to Sandbanks and some Christmas fare. Before his tirade, Redknapp had admitted that Merson had been struggling for

Merson - clearly unfit but raced half the length of the field to give Pompey the lead.

the last five games because of his foot injury. There was no chance of a rest, however. Pompey needed him. Trevor Francis put it all in perspective, feeling, as Joe Royle had done, that perhaps his team should have won. But he added: "I wouldn't be surprised if Portsmouth and Leicester didn't stay at the top. It's a remarkable number of points already and a credit to Harry and Jim."

Portsmouth (3-4-1-2): Hislop; Primus, Foxe, De Zeeuw; Crowe (Harper 81), Diabate (O'Neil 57), Quashie, Taylor; Merson; Todorov, Burton (Pericard 58).
Subs (not used): Kawaguchi, Burchill.
Goal: Merson (27).
Booked: Foxe.
Crystal Palace (3-5-2): Kolinko; Symons, Powell, Popovic; Butterfield, Mullins, Derry, Riihilahti, Gray; Adebola, Black (Akinbiyi 62).
Subs (not used): Michopoulos, Williams, Routledge, Borrowdale.
Goal: Gray (30).
Attendance: 19,217.
Referee: L Cable (Surrey).

Christmas it may have been but there was no sense of a holiday at Fratton Park. Harry was still moving players out and attempting to move others in, although there was a sense of surprise when he made it clear that Mark Burchill was no longer wanted. Burchill was still only 22 and a full international but, with the arrival of Burton, he had fallen down the order of strikers and there did not appear to be a future for him. He had only four months ago begun his recovery from a knee injury similar to that sustained by Bradbury. Redknapp said: "Mark needs to go somewhere to play. I would listen to offers for him." That somewhere turned out to be Dundee. Jim Duffy knew what Burchill could do and readily agreed to take him back over the border, initially on loan. As for Merson, he looked at the end of his tether after the

Mark Burchill - the Scottish international returned over the border to Dundee.

Palace match, his foot injury causing him so much grief that he struggled to walk at times. "The ankle is not right," he said. "I am hobbling badly and I can't move. I'm not enjoying my football and the sooner it is sorted out the better. I've had about ten or 15 injections and I can't carry on doing that. I need to rest it." With a big match at Nottingham Forest two days away and a certain fixture at Old Trafford coming up soon afterwards, it was a bad time to lose your best player.

DOING A WOLVES

Saturday, December 28

NOTTINGHAM FOREST 1
PORTSMOUTH 2

Paul Hart's young side were right up among the play-off challengers, so it was hardly a fixture to relish at the end of a difficult month in which four matches had been drawn. It became even less appetising when Merson was omitted for his own good. But as Pompey were to do so often, they managed to produce a top class result out of adversity. Sky TV's presence meant an evening kick-off and, in 21-goal David Johnson, Forest had a player well capable of reversing the opening-day defeat at Fratton Park. Ex-Forest star Stone was also missing with a hamstring injury but in Linvoy Primus, Pompey had the man of the hour. Rising to the crisis splendidly, Primus marked Johnson out of the game while Quashie, wearing the captain's armband against his old club, led by determined example. Burton and Quashie went close as Pompey dominated from the start and Forest were fortunate to go in at half-time on level terms. Pompey were firmly in command and they got the goal they deserved in spectacular style. O'Neil won the ball on the half-way line and found Taylor on the left. The young wing-back surprised the Forest defence by cutting inside on to his right foot and curling a powerful shot beyond Darren Ward. As Forest found out, Taylor might favour his left but he is by no means one-footed. This knocked the stuffing out of Forest and three minutes from time Ward spilled a Crowe shot for Pericard to ram in the rebound. Michael Dawson set up an interesting injury time by pulling a goal back with a header, but there was no doubt Pompey had shown the watching TV world that even when not at full strength and without key

Linvoy Primus - man of the match against Forest.

players, they could still win - and win well.

Nottingham Forest (4-3-1-2): Ward; Louis-Jean (Thompson 45), Dawson, Walker (Doig 15), Brennan; Prutton, Williams, Reid; Lester (Westcarr 78), Johnson.
Subs (not used): Roche, Bopp.
Goal: Dawson (90).
Booked: Johnson.
Portsmouth (3-5-2): Hislop; Primus, Foxe, De Zeeuw; Harper (Crowe 86), O'Neil, Diabate, Quashie, Taylor; Todorov, Burton (Pericard 80).
Subs (not used): Kawaguchi, Robinson, Burchill.
Goals: Taylor (56), Pericard (87).
Booked: Taylor.
Attendance: 28,165.
Referee: C Foy (Merseyside).

Redknapp, a keen punter but aware of strict league rules governing betting, said afterwards he was glad for a friend who had backed Pompey to win the title when the odds in the summer were 33-1. "We have got a fantastic chance of getting into the premier league. But there are no certainties and there is half a season to play for." So 2002 came to a close. What a calendar year it had been for the club and its supporters. They waited for the dawning of 2003 unbeaten in ten games and 12 points ahead of Sheffield United in third place. The Blades were due at Fratton Park early in the New Year but first there was the little matter of Old Trafford and the FA Cup.

TOP 6 AT END OF DECEMBER 2002

	P	W	D	L	F	A	Pts
PORTSMOUTH	26	17	7	2	52	24	58
Leicester City	26	16	6	4	41	24	54
Sheffield United	25	13	7	5	37	24	46
Norwich City	26	12	7	7	37	23	43
Nottingham Forest	26	12	6	8	41	26	42
Reading	25	13	3	9	26	21	42

9

LIFE AT THE TOP

MANCHESTER UNITED WAS still the talk of the city and beyond as buoyant Pompey entered the New Year hardly daring to believe how far the club had progressed in the last six months. But first there was the difficult trip to Watford for the New Year's Day fixture. Sky TV loved Pompey at this stage of the season, choosing their matches for transmission at every available opportunity. The money this generated was more than handy and it gave Redknapp's side a national profile they had never before enjoyed. So it was at Vicarage Road, an evening kick-off a small price to pay on a wet and miserable start to 2003. Some matches had been called off during the day and the clash between Reading and Leicester had been abandoned at half-time. Had Pompey's match kicked off at 3pm, as was originally scheduled, it too might have been a victim of the weather.

Fratton Park - would this be the home of Premiership football in 2003?

SLEEPING GIANT AWAKES

Wednesday, January 1

**WATFORD 2
PORTSMOUTH 2**

Steve Stone and Paul Merson were deemed fit again but Harry Redknapp decided not to risk them on the heavy surface. They were left on the bench as Pompey sustained a major setback within two minutes when De Zeeuw blocked Heidar Helguson and sustained knee ligament damage but, driven on by captain Quashie in midfield, it was Pompey who dominated the first half. Goalless at the break, it was something of a surprise when Micah Hyde put Watford ahead in the 51st minute. Such was the character in this Pompey side that within three minutes they had equalised, Burton finishing off a move involving Quashie and Harper for his first goal since rejoining the club permanently. Harper had a fine match and deserved the goal of the night in the 58th minute, collecting a pass from Gary O'Neil, sprinting into the area and curling a left foot shot past goalkeeper Chamberlain. For once, Pompey could not hold on and nine minutes from time Neil Cox was unmarked when he headed in Helguson's flick. Had De Zeeuw been on the pitch the defence might not have been so generous.

Kevin Harper - the goal of the night and a booking for the influential midfielder.

Redknapp said: "Once we'd gone ahead a second time I thought we were going to win it. But we got undone at a set piece, which is always disappointing. Credit Watford for the way they came back at us and on balance it was a good point. The state of the pitch wasn't a farce. It was just muddy and the conditions didn't bother us."

Watford (4-4-2): Chamberlain; Ardley, Cox, Gayle, Brown; Pennant (Smith 74), Hyde, Vernazza (Nielsen 73), Robinson (McNamee 66); Noel-Williams, Helguson.
Subs (not used): Lee, Mahon.
Goals: Hyde (51), Cox (81).

LIFE AT THE TOP

Portsmouth (3-5-2): Hislop; Primus, Foxe, De Zeeuw (Crowe 6); Harper, O'Neil, Diabate, Quashie, Taylor; Todorov (Merson 80), Burton (Pericard 60).
Subs (not used): Kawaguchi, Stone.
Goals: Burton (54), Harper (58).
Booked: Harper.
Attendance: 15,048.
Referee: P Rejer (Worcestershire).

Efstathios Tavlaridis - the powerful Greek defender loaned from Arsenal.

De Zeeuw's injury looked to be serious so the ever-busy Redknapp set about finding a replacement in time for the trip to Manchester United. It was not going to be easy and time was running out. Some candidates from the lower divisions might already be cup-tied while other clubs, higher in status, would be unlikely to allow players to join Pompey on loan all the while they, too, were still in the Cup. As it happened, Redknapp took in a reserve match between Tottenham and Arsenal and it was there that he spotted Efstathios Tavlaridis, a 22-year old powerfully-built Greek defender. Tavlaridis was part of Arsenal's huge squad but it would have needed an injury list of epidemic proportions for him to have played in the Gunners' first team. Arsene Wenger was only too pleased to come to Pompey's aid in their hour of need as the countdown to Old Trafford began. Tavlaridis signed on the dotted line and was told to get himself ready for a baptism he would never forget.

Two days before the big match, Pompey lost legendary winger Peter Harris, who died at his home in Hayling Island from a heart attack at the age of 77. Harris would certainly have known what it was like to play at an Old Trafford full house. He did so often enough in his own playing career, a career which was spent entirely with his home city club, building up a formidable record of 211 goals in 514 matches from 1946 to 1960. During the championship seasons of 1949 and 1950 he scored 39 goals and in any other era would surely have earned more than two England caps, but he was unfortunate his own prime coincided with that of Stanley Matthews and Tom Finney, two of the greatest players ever to have appeared for England. Harris held a special place in the hearts of Portsmouth fans because he was one of the few players ever to have been produced for England by the city itself. It was fair to say that Harris had lost interest in the game in recent years, hence his decision to sell his medals and other memorabilia a few months before his death. His last appearance on the Fratton Park pitch he once graced with breath-taking speed and trickery down the wings was in October before the Coventry match at an old players' reunion. Those who remembered his massive contribution to the club in its heyday gave him a special cheer when he was introduced to the crowd. He left at half-time, complaining of the cold weather, never to return to the scene of his greatest triumphs.

Even in Harris's day it is hard to imagine a match which induced so much intense build-up and excitement as the FA Cup third round tie at Old Trafford. Perhaps old-timers would recall trains packed to the luggage racks as Pompey fans headed to Wembley for the 1939 final, but for most fans this took some beating. For success-drenched Manchester United this was just about the least interesting match in a long season of far more glamorous fixtures. Juventus and Real Madrid were still to be played and, with due respect,

first division Pompey - even as leaders - did not catch their aristocratic attention. Among the Pompey players there was genuine optimism; Shaka Hislop, part of Redknapp's West Ham team which beat United in the fourth round two years before, reckoned another upset was on the cards. Hislop said: "Harry got the tactics right then and he can get them right again. I believe he can mastermind another cup defeat for United. We are very confident."

Shaka Hislop - confident of a Pompey win at Old Trafford

LIFE AT THE TOP

Rosie Francis, *Portsmouth in the Community* manager, braved the pre-dawn cold of a car park at 2.30am to round up almost 1,000 Pompey fans and herd them aboard a fleet of 18 coaches for a 5am departure. Isle of Wight fans got on to a ferry at much the same time for the long journey north among a total Pompey contingent of 9,000. By Warwickshire the Pompey hordes hit a blizzard, but while some might have been tempted to turn back, the vast majority pressed on and were rewarded when blue skies and sunshine, not typical Manchester weather, greeted their arrival.

Old Trafford holds in excess of 67,000 but the lack of passion and atmosphere in some matches had been compared unfavourably by Sir Alex Ferguson to a morgue. Feeble cries of "United, United" were drowned out by a fantastic reception from Pompey fans when their heroes took the pitch. A massive ticker-tape welcome was accompanied by the Pompey Chimes ringing out from all quarters. It might almost have been a home game, but for the palatial setting, as the 57,000 non-Pompey supporters contemplated their prawn sandwiches in bemused silence. One Portsmouth fan, finding his ticket placed him among banks of United red and white, was pleased to discover in the next seat a man from the Isle of Wight. "Thank goodness, another Pompey fan," he said. "You must be joking," replied his neighbour. "This is my regular seat, I come here every match." They may not be the most vociferous of fans, but United command loyalty from all parts of the world.

Saturday, January 4
FA Cup third round

MANCHESTER UNITED 4
PORTSMOUTH 1

The fans had played their part, now it was up to the players. This was a big test for Pompey in discovering just how good they could be. A noon kick-off for television purposes meant Pompey's match was being played before other third round ties so that briefly they were the centre of attention for the whole country. If Pompey were to go on and be promoted, they would be meeting clubs like United as equals in a few months' time, but a heavy defeat would indicate much work still to be done to close the gap in class and expectation. So there was more to this meeting than a one-off cup match might otherwise have presented. The absence of De Zeeuw gave Tavlaridis the chance to make his debut, while old hands Stone and Merson were just the sort of people needed for these sort of big occasions and were restored to the starting line-up. Pompey needed a calm, steady start - and they did not get it. Within four minutes United were ahead. Van Nistelrooy found space on the edge of the area and slipped a pass to Ryan Giggs, who was sent sprawling by Primus's desperate lunge. Hislop went the wrong way from van Nistelrooy's spot-kick and suddenly Pompey were a goal behind.

Nervous Pompey looked vulnerable every time United poured forward and, when Diabate's crashing tackle on Gary Neville conceded a free-kick 25 yards out, gold-emblazoned fans were temporarily silenced as a certain David Beckham sized up his options. Beckham free-kicks from just such a range and position have been the stuff of eulogies all around the footballing globe. As away fans gulped in anticipation, Beckham unleashed a trademark effort, curling beyond Hislop and into the top corner. A stunning goal, and for Pompey it was getting embarrassing. Two down and only 17 minutes played, the talk among fans concerned damage limitation, not of stirring responses. Tavlaridis, coming to terms with the ultimate in hostile debuts, gave away another free-kick from a similar range, but this time Beckham could only hit the woodwork. Chants of "we're going to win 3-2" helped maintain morale at a time when it was badly required but suddenly Pompey began to settle, perhaps

as United realised even before half-time they had already done enough to win. United's complacency was shattered in the 38th minute when Pompey pulled a goal back with their first shot on target. Taylor's long free-kick was headed across goal by Foxe and, as Carroll dithered under a challenge from Todorov, the unmistakable figure of Stone bundled the ball home.

When the players came in at half-time, Redknapp immediately made two changes, sending O'Neil and Pericard on in place of Merson and Diabate and switching to 3-5-2. For the 30 minutes after the resumption it was a different game as Pompey tore into much-vaunted United with a relish and determination they had not shown until Stone's goal. They also revealed a degree of sophistication beyond the first division as United struggled to cope. Taylor shot over from ten yards and went close with another effort and Ferguson, perturbed by the unexpected resistance, sent on Paul Scholes to get a grip in midfield.

The turning point came in the 65th minute and, for every Pompey fan, either at Old Trafford or at home watching it on television, the moment will be forever etched in the mind. Like a slow-motion nightmare, every step of Nigel Quashie's run from the half-way line on to O'Neil's pass will be agonisingly familiar to those who witnessed it. Not an

LIFE AT THE TOP

Scenes from the "Theatre of Dreams" -
Above: Captain Quashie takes control despite the close
attention of David Beckham.
Below: Hayden Foxe fouls Ruud van Nistelrooy
to concede another penalty.

Matt Taylor cuts Beckham down to size.

opponent in sight, on he went, roared on by the crowd. The ball was on his favoured left foot, Carroll was coming from his line without much conviction...a chip or a blast, what should he do? In the split-second it takes to make such a life-changing decision Quashie chose neither. As Old Trafford held its breath, Quashie lifted the ball on to the terraces, Pompey's one gilt-edged chance of equalising and changing the course of the match gone forever. Quashie sank to his knees in disbelief, and a reprieved United, woken from their lethargy, ruthlessly punished his error. Giggs sent van Nistelrooy into the area and, although Foxe seemed to have hustled the Dutch striker away from danger, a trailing leg sent him crashing to the ground. Another penalty and another van Nistelrooy goal.

United heaved a sigh of relief but even then the action wasn't over. Todorov thought he had pulled a goal back but he was denied by a linesman's flag for offside. In injury time, Scholes got away from Tavlaridis, though he too looked offside, before chipping a shot over Hislop. It was a score which undeniably flattered United but it was a reminder to Pompey that, even when catching them on an off-day, Ferguson's men had still scored four times.

At least Pompey "won" the off-field jousting, consistently out-singing the home fans although numerically swamped. Even Beckham applauded the Pompey fans as they sang "we'll be back next year" at the start of the long journey home, but there were some salutary lessons to be learned, as Redknapp acknowledged: "For the first 20 minutes United's movement and passing were scary. The lads were a bit nervous in the first half but once we scored, their self-belief returned. At half-time they reckoned they could have a go at them. I told them to pass it through midfield as we normally do instead of knocking it long. In the second half we looked like the side to score next. We looked a good side and in control of the game for long periods. I thought there was an equaliser there for us, and who knows what would have happened if we had got it. If Quashie had scored then you could have said we were on our way for sure. You fancy Nigel in those situations. He is a great striker of the ball with both feet and normally buries those type of chances. It was a good education for the lads who have never played at Manchester United before but there is no point kidding yourself. If you don't take your chances against a side like United you will lose. They are on a different level."

Ferguson offered words of consolation, believing Pompey would be promoted as champions: "Pompey impressed me. Their fans came up in numbers and helped make it a good FA Cup atmosphere. I didn't think it was a 4-1 scoreline but in the first half it looked as if it would go that way. We went to sleep for their goal and it lifted them and their supporters and in the second half they made it hard for us." In statistical terms Pompey had failed to reach the fourth round for the fourth successive season. But while defeat was by the same margin, it was an altogether different occasion to that at Fratton Park exactly a year earlier when Pompey were eliminated in such abject fashion by Leyton Orient, a team at the time described by their own manager as not even a very good third division side.

Manchester United (4-4-2): Carroll; G Neville, Ferdinand, Blanc, Silvestre (Brown 82); Beckham, Keane (Stewart 45), P Neville, Richardson (Scholes 59); van Nistelrooy, Giggs.
Subs (not used): Ricardo, Forlan.
Goals: van Nistelrooy (4, 81 pens), Beckham (17), Scholes (90).
Portsmouth (3-5-1-1): Hislop; Primus, Foxe, Tavlaridis; Harper, Stone (Burton 88), Diabate (Pericard 45), Quashie, Taylor; Merson (O'Neil 45); Todorov.
Subs (not used): Kawaguchi, Crowe.
Goal: Stone (38).
Booked: Diabate, Tavlaridis.
Attendance: 67,222.
Referee: P Riley (West Yorkshire).

SLEEPING GIANT AWAKES

Yakubu Ayegbeni or should it be Ayegbeni Yakubu? Or, as a variation, what about Yacubu Aiyegbeni? No one was quite sure what his name was or the spelling when the Nigerian from Israel showed up at Pompey for training before the formalisation of his loan signing. Redknapp took the opportunity while at Old Trafford to ask Sir Alex what he thought of the powerful and quick 20-year-old striker who had scored one of the goals in Maccabi Haifa's 3-0 Champions League win over an admittedly weakened Manchester United. Ferguson raved about him, suggesting he would be Pompey's best signing to date. With that sort of recommendation, Pompey set about the business of registering him, hoping to succeed where Derby had failed only six months previously in obtaining a work permit. Yakubu (we'll call him that for the time being) arrived at the club's training ground in some secrecy. Until the work permit was obtained, he could not take part in any of the club's activities, and that included training, so it was a question of applying and waiting. As Yakubu settled into temporary accommodation at the Marriott Hotel at Paulsgrove, he was joined there by Markus Heikkinen, a Finnish international defender who had been signed for the rest of the season as cover on a trial basis. The Pompey of January 2003 had a real international flavour about it and showed the extent of Redknapp and Smith's scouting network and contacts. As if they were not enough, Pompey were back in the hunt for Tim Sherwood from St Albans, Hertfordshire.

Markus Heikkinen - his arrival augmented the international flavour of Redknapp's squad.

Yakubu Ayegbeni, or is that Ayegbeni Yakubu, arrives.

SLEEPING GIANT AWAKES

Monday, January 13

PORTSMOUTH 1
SHEFFIELD UNITED 2

This important match should have been played on the Saturday but frost put paid to that and, with paymasters Sky demanding a quick re-arrangement, the match was put back to Monday. So the television cameras were again in evidence (how they loved Pompey) and their perserverance was rewarded with a match of high-class entertainment. Sheffield United were on a roll, 13 matches unbeaten, which had taken them into third place in the table, the semi-finals of the Worthington Cup and to the fourth round of the FA Cup. A few days before Neil Warnock's side had beaten Liverpool 2-1 in the first leg of the Worthington Cup semi-final. Here, then, were formidable opponents, the one side realistically likely to break the Portsmouth-Leicester stranglehold on the automatic promotion placings. The fact that Sheffield United's attention and resources were diverted so often by cup competitions worked in favour of the division's top two. Pompey themselves were un-

Nigel Quashie and Sheffield United's Robert Page show the pain of a full-blooded clash.

beaten in eleven matches and a win over United would have widened the gap between top and third to 16 points. The punishment for losing was as severe. The gap would have been ten points and United would have two games in hand. So, by any standards, this was a big night and Pompey were handed a pre-match boost when Gianluca Festa returned from two months on the injured list earlier than expected.

Pompey had their chances early in the match, the irrepressible Taylor at the centre of most of them with those familiar probing, all-action runs down the left, but it was United who took the lead in the 24th minute. Michael Tonge, a dominant figure on the left side of midfield, set up Peter Ndlovu for the opener and although O'Neil hit the woodwork, there was enough concern in the Pompey camp to change their system to 4-3-1-2 for the second half. Almost immediately, Pericard struck a post, Quashie was inches away and Merson rattled the bar with a 25-yard free-kick. Just when it seemed Pompey would never score, Todorov set up O'Neil for the equaliser. This set up a pulsating last 15 minutes in which Pompey were denied a penalty when Robert Page appeared to handle Pericard's header before United snatched a late winner. Tavlaridis, who had replaced Festa, and Foxe were at fault as

O'Neil and Todorov celebrate the equaliser - but it wasn't enough.

Michael Brown fired home. How ironic that Brown spent four matches on loan with Pompey when Alan Ball was manager and was sent back to Manchester City when Bally was not convinced of his commitment to the Pompey cause.

Redknapp, of course, realised the implications of defeat and the potential damage: "It was criminal. We got ourselves into a position to win but threw it away. We had a nailed-on penalty turned down and then gave them a soft winner. People have got to learn to head the ball away from danger instead of trying to be clever. But it goes that way sometimes. Sheffield United are a good side but in the second half I could see only one winner." Warnock, that most unpredictable of managers, bathed in the glory of being only the second side to win at Fratton Park in the league: "I have been dying to bring a good side to Portsmouth for ages. I love it here. I love how intimidating it is and I love the Pompey Chimes when they ring out. I don't think anyone deserved to lose, both sides showed lots of skill. A draw would have been fairer."

Portsmouth (3-4-1-2): Hislop; Primus, Foxe, Festa (Tavlaridis 76); Stone (Harper 72), O'Neil, Quashie, Taylor; Merson; Todorov (Burton 86), Pericard.
Subs (not used): Kawaguchi, Diabate.
Goal: O'Neil (78).
Sheffield United (4-4-2): Kenny; Jagielka, Murphy, Page, Quinn; Montgomery, Brown, McCall, Tonge; Ndlovu, Allison.
Subs (not used): Kozluk, Ten Heuval, Kabba, Smith, Peschisolido.
Goals: Ndlovu (24), Brown (87).
Booked: Brown, Quinn.
Attendance: 18,872.
Referee: C Wilkes (Gloucestershire).

For Merson, the Sheffield United setback was something of a watershed. Booed by a section of fans as he laboured to find the form which had so thrilled all supporters before Christmas, he

decided on the spur of the moment to quit the club, only to be dissuaded from such drastic action by a combination of his wife and the manager. Merson said: "I wasn't going to come back. I got on the phone to my wife and the manager after the game and told them I'd had enough. I was that upset." Luckily for Pompey, Redknapp was at his persuasive best and publicly declared his belief that in time Merson would rediscover his quality, but fans should be patient.

New Year Blues - booed by a section of the crowd after a lapse in the exceptional form he had shown before Christmas, Paul Merson decided to quit and then changed his mind.

Meanwhile, Pompey's secret weapon Yakubu was about to get his work permit. Married to a Portuguese girl, which he was not when on trial at Derby, there was now no barrier to his precious document, but he still had to go abroad and then re-enter Britain for his passport to be stamped. So much for red tape, now for Brighton and Hove Albion. Before that, something had to be done about his name. The number 20 shirt had been allocated for him but what to put on the back? Eventually it was settled on YAKUBU, although the newspapers continued throughout the remainder of the season to call him Yakubu or Ayegbeni without knowing which was right. Fans called him 'The Yak' and that was that. Not that any of this bothered him. He said: "I am looking forward to playing my first match. I have been very impressed by my new teammates and by the supporters. I have always wanted to play in England and I am delighted to join Portsmouth. I believe I can score the goals to take them into the Premiership. This is my ambition, to play in the Premiership and I hope to do it with Portsmouth." Pompey agreed to pay around £300,000 to keep him on loan for the rest of the season, a small outlay if his goals went some way to guaranteeing promotion.

'The Yak' prepares to unleash himself on an unsuspecting first division.

Saturday, January 18

**BRIGHTON 1
PORTSMOUTH 1**

Pools experts would have had this down as a cast-iron away win. Pompey were at the top and Brighton at the bottom. But while Pompey were not quite the force of before Christmas, Brighton, under the shrewd management of Steve Coppell, were much improved. Two major factors also mitigated against Pompey. The cramped Withdean

SLEEPING GIANT AWAKES

Former Pompey defender Robbie Pethick clashes with Nigel Quashie in a tough battle at the Withdean Stadium.

Stadium, a converted athletics venue, reduced the capacity and the atmosphere and Pompey's travelling army was down to the first 800 who could obtain tickets. A midday kick-off did not help either and those fans prevented from making the 50-mile journey watched a giant screen at Fratton Park instead.

Revitalised Brighton tore into Pompey, hustling them into mistakes and making it difficult to get their passing game together. Stone limped off with a recurrence of his hamstring trouble and Todorov had a penalty appeal rejected in attempting to go around Ben Roberts. Redknapp gave the players a verbal lashing at half-time, but it was Brighton who went ahead in the 54th minute, Paul Brooker finding leading scorer Bobby Zamora, who twisted away from a couple of defensive challenges to score with a low shot. Yakubu came on three minutes later to loud cheers and almost scored immediately, his shot being parried by Roberts for Guy Butters to clear. But the equaliser was not long in coming. Inevitably, Taylor and Merson were involved, as they had been so often in the past, Todorov completing the job.

Redknapp was none-too-impressed by the Withdean Stadium, Brighton's seemingly permanent temporary home: "It was like playing at Sutton United in the FA Cup. Look where our fans were, stuck up in the corner of the ground in the middle of nowhere. It was a fair result and another away point. We are drawing at the moment but not losing. Good luck to Brighton. They have got spirit and work hard so they have a chance of staying up." The point gained grew in importance and value when a few hours later Leicester lost 3-2 at Gillingham.

Brighton (3-5-2): Roberts; Pethick, Cullip, Mayo; Watson, Brooker, Carpenter, Oatway (Blackwell 79), Jones; Barrett (Kitson 82), Zamora.
Subs (not used): Packham, Hart, Piercy.
Goal: Zamora (54).
Booked: Watson.
Portsmouth (3-4-1-2): Hislop; Primus, Foxe, Tavlaridis (Crowe 69); Stone (Harper 38), Diabate, Quashie, Taylor; Merson; Todorov, Pericard (Yakubu 57).
Subs (not used): Kawaguchi, Burton.
Goal: Todorov (64).
Booked: Stone, Tavlaridis.
Attendance: 6,848.
Referee: M Messias (North Yorkshire).

Two months later, reflecting on the season as it neared its end, Brighton's Coppell singled out his three best players of the first division. His first was Michael Brown of Sheffield United, Michael Dawson of Nottingham Forest was his second and his third was Merson. He said of him: "Portsmouth have come from the wilderness. Last season they were right down at the bottom, but from day one this season they have been right up there. Paul Merson was the difference between mediocrity and being special, particularly early on. His quality and skill in that floating role gave them something extra. He was instrumental in so many of their goals in the first third of the season. He was not so effective later because teams have seen the way Portsmouth play and kept him quiet. But if he goes into the Premiership next season, treating it as his swansong, then he can undoubtedly still make a big impact."

As Coppell said, teams had started to work out where Pompey were dangerous and who made them tick. It did not take a genius to see that Merson was a key figure and it was one of the reasons why Redknapp pursued the signature of Tottenham's Tim Sherwood with such vigour. Once Tottenham had at last cleared the way, there was interest in him from West Bromwich Albion of the Prem-

The signing of Tim Sherwood from Spurs was to relieve the burden on Paul Merson.

iership. The deal with Pompey was on, then off and then on again. Spurs would receive £200,000 if Pompey went up and Sherwood, with a parting swipe at Hoddle, joined Pompey for the remainder of the season, determined to finish a personally disappointing campaign with a championship medal. Having led Blackburn into the top flight, he knew what he was talking about.

In time, once he had regained the edge of match fitness, Sherwood lifted the burden from Merson, using his many years in the Premiership and the experience of a couple of England caps to become Pompey's second play-maker. With Yakubu banging in goals against Barnet and Southend reserves in his own quest for fitness, their double signing added a whole new dimension to Pompey and with perfect timing. Luckily, the Brighton match was Pompey's last for two weeks and the opportunity was taken for rest and recreation. Merson limped off to Barbados for a few days sunshine, played some tennis, grew a beard and came home refreshed for battles ahead. Back at Fratton Park, Steve Stone discovered the extent of his hamstring injury and six weeks out of action was diagnosed, while Mark Burchill alerted Jim Duffy's Dundee to his availability by scoring a hat-trick in the reserves, albeit against Barnet's second string. A deal was imminent.

Richard Hughes - the struggle to recover from a hamstring injury was compounded by a portakabin door!

Meanwhile, Richard Hughes's season went from bad to worse. Only now recovering from a persistent hamstring injury, the Scottish under-21 international had so far been restricted in his appearances to a handful of games. Then, at the training

ground, a portakabin door, swinging in the wind, slammed shut on his finger and sliced off the tip. Later, in an effort to get him back to full fitness, he was sent to Grimsby on loan. Never rains but it pours.

So, January ended with Pompey collecting only two points from three league matches, but they were still top. Renewed by their week off, Pompey's players returned fresh and eager to finish off a job they had started so successfully. There was a long way to go.

TOP 6 AT END OF JANUARY 2003

	P	W	D	L	F	A	Pts
PORTSMOUTH	**29**	**17**	**9**	**3**	**56**	**29**	**60**
Leicester City	29	17	7	5	46	28	58
Sheffield United	27	15	7	5	42	26	52
Nottingham Forest	29	12	9	8	44	29	45
Norwich City	28	12	8	8	39	26	44
Coventry City	29	11	10	8	36	32	43

10

DERBY DAYS

GOING INTO FEBRUARY, ALL was not completely well in the Pompey camp, at least in terms of results. There had been a noticeable tailing-off, particularly at home where visiting sides had packed defences, sat on Merson and taken tactical steps, where possible, to restrict Taylor's defence-wrecking runs down the left. But if Pompey were enduring something of a hiccup, the good news was that no other team was taking advantage. Leicester were, as usual, dogging Pompey's every step but, far more importantly, none of the chasing pack below the top two teams was proving capable of stringing together enough wins to apply any pressure. Reading had their moments, Sheffield United were inconsistent, Norwich were unable to sustain some positive results, Nottingham Forest and Wolves threatened but then fell away and Ipswich were leaving their expected run to the play-offs later and later. Derby and Coventry, two teams expected to be among the contenders, were nearer the bottom than the top so the fact that Pompey had not

won at Fratton Park for more than two months almost did not matter. None of their rivals was capable of manoeuvring into a position to challenge Pompey's proud placing at the top of the first division. Still, the sooner normal service was resumed the better and the visit of Grimsby was the perfect occasion to put behind them (comparative) recent struggles.

Saturday, February 1

**PORTSMOUTH 3
GRIMSBY TOWN 0**

Yakubu and Tim Sherwood made their home debuts and Redknapp urged his players to get back to their pre-Christmas form. It was Yakubu who quelled any nerves with a goal in the fourth minute, leaving John McDermott for dead with an electrifying burst of speed before slipping a shot under Danny Coyne. Yakubu's goal saw all the old confidence flowing back and Coyne kept beleaguered Grimsby alive with first-half saves from Merson, Quashie and Sherwood. But the longer the battling

'The Yak' opens his account against Grimsby.

Mariners kept it down to one goal, the more edgy Pompey became and it might have been different had player-manager Paul Groves not spurned a clear chance to equalise. There were only 15 minutes remaining when Taylor's low cross from the left was turned into his own net by defender Simon Ford. The match was deep into stoppage time when Quashie rounded off a Merson pass.

Redknapp recognised that the match had not produced one of Pompey's better performances but it had brought three more points. He said: "We needed the second goal to kill the game. If Grimsby had equalised it would have been game on." But the real plus point, as far as Redknapp was concerned, was the calming performance of Sherwood in midfield. Sherwood's authority had made the six-month transfer negotiations seem worthwhile while Yakubu hinted at a world class talent-in-the-making.

Redknapp added: "He started like Thierry Henry in the first 20 minutes; he was on fire. He's lightning quick and got real pace. We've got to get him on the ball more and make him understand that defenders are frightened of him. If he runs at them, he'll be a problem for any defence in the division. If this was horse racing I'd say he'll come on for the run." Sherwood,

shaking off too long in the Spurs reserves, found Yakubu equally exhilarating: "I thought he was on a motor bike," he said. Grimsby's harassed defenders would not have disagreed.

Portsmouth (3-4-1-2): Hislop; Primus, Foxe (Diabate 90), Tavlaridis; Harper (Crowe 85), Sherwood, Quashie, Taylor; Merson; Yakubu (Pericard 90), Todorov.
Subs (not used): Kawaguchi, Burton.
Goals: Yakubu (4), Ford (og 75), Quashie (90).
Grimsby (4-5-1): Coyne; McDermott, Chettle, Ford, Gallimore; Campbell, Groves, Santos (Ward 88), Bolder (Soames 78), Mansaram; Livingstone.
Subs (not used): Allaway, Cooke, Parker.
Booked: Mansaram.
Attendance: 19,428.
Referee: A Bates (Staffordshire).

Milan Mandaric - with victory in sight, he wanted to get into the Premiership with all guns blazing.

Milan Mandaric, fears placated by Pompey's ultimately convincing win, had his contribution to Pompey's surge to the front door of the Premiership recognised the next day when he received a Lifetime Achievement Award from the city's newspaper, The News. The award paid tribute to sporting excellence, dedication and commitment. The chairman was in magnanimous mood, praising lifetime fans John Westwood and Joyce Tynan, both of whom were present: "This award has got as much to do with the Pompey fans as me. Fans like John and Joyce who have followed us through the dark days into better times. This award is so special to me because I feel part of this great community."

Excellence, dedication and commitment might also have described Linvoy Primus's season. Had Eddie Howe been fit, Primus might not have enjoyed as many first team games as he had so far but, given the opportunity, he had developed, perhaps even to Redknapp's surprise, into an integral part of Pompey's rock-like defence. Twice Pompey fans voted him Player of the Month and then came the prestigious Nationwide Division One Player of the Month award from a poll conducted across the country. The former Reading defender was playing as well as at any time in his career and Redknapp recognised his

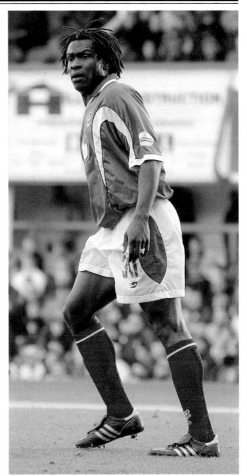

Linvoy Primus - rock-solid in defence and his efforts rewarded by the fans.

development by offering him an extension of his contract. For Howe, the man he replaced on the right side of defence, the news was less impressive. His contribution to Pompey's eminence so far limited to five minutes, a specialist gave him the advice he had been dreading: No more football for you this season. With that, he headed to the

United States for an operation designed to rectify his knee problems but bitterly disappointed not to have been able to play any significant part in Pompey's astonishing season. Tavlaridis, adjusting nicely after the traumas of his Old Trafford debut, agreed to stay on for a second month, while Carl Robinson headed for Sheffield Wednesday and later Walsall on loan after losing his place in the squad.

There was news also of the death of yet another member of Pompey's great past when Phil Rookes died in East Anglia at the age of 82. Rookes would have

The death of Phil Rookes, another Pompey hero from the glory days, was a reminder of how far the club still had to go.

been proud, like Peter Harris, to have seen his old club on the verge of reclaiming their place among football's elite. When he was a Pompey player, the club were a power in the land although his career was ruined by World War II, which took six years from his prime. At 19 and fresh from Bradford City, he played his second match for Pompey in the fifth round of the FA Cup against West Ham in front of a crowd of 47,614. After the war he returned to Fratton Park and was the regular right-back for three years during which time Pompey won the championship in 1949. Later he joined Colchester and managed Sussex League Chichester. There was a certain irony in his death and that of Harris just when Pompey were so close to success, and a reminder that it is one thing to get into the top division, it is another to win it as Rookes and Harris had done. Twice.

Saturday, February 8

PORTSMOUTH 6
DERBY COUNTY 2

If the win over Grimsby had not been fluent or decisive, the victory over Derby was all that management and supporters could have wished for. When the fixtures were first announced, this would have been seen as one of the best but when Derby came to

Fratton Park they were a pale shadow - even of the team relegated from the Premiership. Deon Burton had gone to Pompey, Malcolm Christie and Chris Riggott to Middlesbrough, Mart Poom to Sunderland and Danny Higginbotham to Southampton, all just to ease the wage bill. Morale was patently at a low ebb and it was not Pompey's business to feel any more than a passing sympathy. Nor did they, as Derby were ruthlessly swept aside in a first half performance of devastating power and precision, laying the foundations for the biggest home win since March 1992 when Millwall were sent packing 6-1.

John Gregory, later to be suspended by Derby, was left in particular to rue the failure to sign Yakubu the previous summer after a successful trial at Pride Park. Derby were unable to obtain a work permit for him because he had not played enough matches for Nigeria. Now, as a Pompey player, "The Yak" ran riot, netting twice and helping to create three more. Derby gamely got the score back to 3-2 at one stage but fell apart

Merson converts Yakubu's cross to start the goal feast.

near the end under Pompey's incessant attacking onslaught. There was no stopping Pompey once Merson had converted Yakubu's cross at the second attempt, the first hitting the bar, and in the 17th minute Pompey were two up when Harper and Taylor combined for the Nigerian to score. Taylor gave another breathtaking example of his qual-

ity when he raced on to Todorov's pass to beat Lee Grant. Three down after 22 minutes, it could not get any worse for John Gregory, surely. But it did. The former Pompey boss had already been taunted by chants of "Gregory out" from both sets of fans but early in the second half he was dismissed from the dugout after a row with match officials.

Yakubu proved a handful for the Derby defence all afternoon and combined with Todorov to produce three late goals.

From his new vantage point in the stands, Gregory saw Derby produce a Kinkladze-inspired mini-revival. Kinkladze's shot was parried by Hislop for Lee Morris to follow up and then, after Todorov fouled Warren Barton, the little master put away the penalty. But Yakubu and Todorov combined to set up three late goals to leave the Derby defence floundering and humiliated.

Redknapp acknowledged his team's attacking desire and the flair that brought them six goals: "I only have three players at the back who are defensively-minded. The rest like to bomb forward and it can be exciting to watch. That's the way we play and we can't complain. We got three goals last week and six this playing in that manner." If there were any doubts about Pompey's durability, they must have been dispelled for all but the most pessimistic by these two results. Pompey were not about to fold.

Portsmouth (3-4-1-2): Hislop; Primus, Foxe, Tavlaridis (Heikinnen 90); Harper, Sherwood, Quashie (Diabate 88), Taylor; Merson; Yakubu, Todorov.
Subs (not used): Kawaguchi, Pericard, Burton.
Goals: Merson (3), Yakubu (17, 80), Taylor (22), Todorov (73, 85).
Booked: Tavlaridis, Sherwood.
Derby (4-4-2): Grant; Barton, Evatt, Elliott, Zavagno; Bolder, Lee, Kinkladze, Boertien; Morris, McLeod.
Subs (not used): Oakes, Jackson, Ravanelli, Murray, Tudgay.
Goals: Morris (58), Kinkladze (67 pen).
Booked: Elliott, Boertien.
Attendance: 19,503.
Referee: C Penton (Sussex).

Little wonder that Pompey took the first available opportunity to reach an agreement with Maccabi Haifa to have first refusal on the player's signature when it became available in the summer. The Israeli club believed they had on their books one of the world's brightest forward prospects and they wanted to make sure they were properly recompensed. Glenn Hoddle of Tottenham and Gordon Strachan of Southampton both made personal checks on Yakubu in the wake of his startling early performances but were not convinced that, at £4m, Yakubu could make the same sort of impact in the Premiership at his age and stage of development. Not that Pompey were committed to paying the £4m, but it was as well to be at the head of any potential queue. Redknapp liked what he saw of Yakubu in those early stages: "Yakubu is a player of fantastic potential but he is still only a young lad. His pace is scary. He can hit the ball with both feet and can take a knock as well." Later he pleaded with fans to be patient because there were some matches where he was unable to stamp his authority in quite the same way as he had done in his first few appearances: "Fans have got to realise he's still learning. We are trying to teach him where and when to make runs. But it takes time."

Merson, meanwhile, was looking the better for his mid-season rest, beard or no beard. Rejuvenated by his break, he went on record to say that if Pompey were promoted he would like another crack at the Premiership with them. No doubt he was looking forward to a trip to Aston Villa.

And still Redknapp's signing spree was showing no signs of slowing down. Worried that Kawaguchi was his only experienced cover for Hislop, Redknapp signed Sasa Ilic, the Australian-born Yugoslavian international goalkeeper whose journey around some of football's more deserted outposts had taken him from St Leonard's Stamcroft in Sussex to Zalaegerszeg in Hungary in five years. Ilic reached the Premiership with Charlton and spent seven matches on loan in 2001-02 at Pompey when Rix was manager. While with the Hungarians he had played against Manchester United in the Champions League but, as the season entered its final, critical phase, Redknapp did not want all the good work to collapse for want of a goalkeeper. Ilic duly signed for the rest of the season and Redknapp announced that at last there would be no more signings. No one believed him with the transfer deadline still six weeks away.

Matt Taylor earned praise from England under-21 boss David Platt for his first appearance at that level and Kevin Harper showed how much he had developed under the auspices of Redknapp and Jim Smith by being named in Scotland's "Future" squad. All of which led to February's big match, not quite a grudge match but a game of such significance that the outcome of the first division title might depend on it. Leicester versus Portsmouth.

Ever since the rain-lashed farce at Fratton Park, Pompey had nursed a grievance. Paul Merson encapsulated that sense of injustice in the wake of Leicester's 2-0 win when he said that, in normal conditions, Pompey's greater flair would enable them to beat Leicester nine times out of ten. For their part, Leicester felt that fuss over the conditions had stopped them getting the recognition their performance deserved. Micky Adams, or should that be Micky-taking Adams, stoked up the flames in the week building up to the return match at the Walkers Stadium by conceding the championship to Pompey. Spotting a cunning piece of gamesmanship, Redknapp laughed it off but, like Adams, he knew this was indeed a fixture out of the ordinary.

The performances of Kevin Harper (right) led Scotland coach Berti Vogts to name him in his "Future" squad.

More seriously, Redknapp revealed that he had feared for his future after turning down the opportunity to manage Leicester when they were still in the Premiership and looking for a replacement for Peter Taylor. Having shaken hands in agreement with the Leicester chairman, Redknapp changed his mind on the journey home and instead became Pompey's director of football, unsure of what that job entailed and thinking that in rejecting Leicester he might never get another opportunity to manage at the top level.

Monday, February 17

LEICESTER CITY 1
PORTSMOUTH 1

Sky Television were in place as usual and there was no sign of any rain as Leicester had the better of the first half, opening the scoring in the ninth minute when James Scowcroft intercepted a clearance by De Zeeuw, freshly restored after six weeks out with knee ligament damage. Pompey struggled to find any semblance of their usual style and resorted uncharacteristically to long balls out of defence, gratefully snaffled by defensive giants Elliott and Taggart. Dickov twice missed clear openings, including a one-on-one with Hislop, before Pompey equalised after the break when Taylor cut in on to his right foot and scored via the inside of a post. Neither side pushed as hard as they might for a winner but Pompey unquestionably finished the stronger, Quashie blasting a free-kick wide in stoppage time. No wonder 2,000 delighted Pompey fans stayed behind at the final whistle to chorus: "We're gonna win the league." Their team had done them proud, again.

Redknapp, aware that revenge had not been taken, was still pleased with the result and especially with Taylor: "Matt's goal was a bit like the one he scored at Nottingham Forest that won us the game up there. Everyone talks about his left foot but he is superb at cutting in from the right. We have seen it so many times this year." There was praise also for the team spirit, a factor which had helped Pompey come through many a crisis already and was to do so again in the future: "The lads never give in. We always seem to come back when we go behind. We came to Leicester to get three points but the important thing is we did not get beaten. Even at 1-0 down I was confident we would get a draw out of the game. We conceded a sloppy goal but we were better when we got the ball down and exploited the space for Kevin Harper."

Leicester (4-4-2): Walker; Sinclair, Elliott, Taggart, Rogers; McKinlay, Izzet, Davidson, Scowcroft; Dickov (Wright 83), Benjamin (Summerbee 74).

Subs (not used): Flowers, Stewart, Jones.
Goal: Benjamin (9).
Booked: Scowcroft, McKinlay.
Portsmouth (3-4-1-2): Hislop; Primus, Foxe,
De Zeeuw; Harper, Sherwood, Quashie,
Taylor; Merson; Yakubu (Pericard 80),
Todorov (Diabate 90).
Subs (not used): Kawaguchi, Festa, O'Neil.
Goal: Taylor (65).
Booked: Quashie.
Attendance: 31,775.
Referee: M Pike (Cumbria).

Kevin Harper's transformation at the age of 27 was one of the unexpected bonuses of the season. Jim Smith had sold him to Tony Pulis in the belief, as he said at the time, that he could take him no further forward at Derby. Until Redknapp came along, Harper had been in and out of the Pompey team, never fully justifying his undoubted talent as a winger of pace and no little skill. His temperament did not help him get the best out of himself, a string of bookings and suspensions preventing him putting together a run of appearances which might have hastened his comparatively late development. But now he was close to the finished article, noted by Scotland's Berti Vogts, and an important part of Redknapp's first team squad. Like Primus, his contribution to the Pompey cause was not expected to be anything other than peripheral at the start of the season, but the offer of a new two-year contract was reward for his newly-found maturity.

Taylor, who must surely have been the bargain of the close sea-son, had Merson fighting his corner again: "I reckon Matt is good enough to play for England now. For years England have been saying they have no left backs but now they have Matt Taylor. I don't see anyone better." Richard Hughes arrived at Fratton Park at the same time and from a similar lower division background. Had he stayed free of injuries Hughes might have made a similar impact but now he was off to Grimsby with a simple desire: To get fit and stay fit with next season and the Premiership in mind.

Saturday, February 22

PORTSMOUTH 1
GILLINGHAM 0

George Best was Pompey's guest, hoping for a better spectacle than on his last visit to Fratton Park when he watched the Leicester wash-out. Not that Gillingham's presence guaranteed an afternoon of fun and frolics. Prompted by evergreen player-manager Andy Hessenthaler, at 37 still one of the division's better players, the Gills were not the sort of side to give in easily. One goal always looked likely to settle a sterile, incident-free match, and so it proved. Pompey did not so much as force a corner in the first half and the large crowd, close to capacity, was strangely subdued. Not that Gillingham ever got close to scoring, or even

SLEEPING GIANT AWAKES

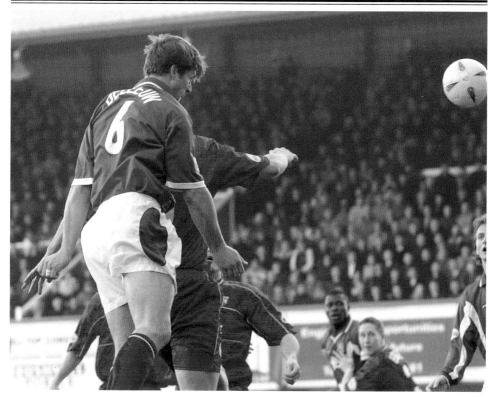

Arjan de Zeeuw rises above the Gillingham defence to score the only goal of a sterile game.

close to the goal. Arjan De Zeeuw, with his first for Pompey, ensured the points with a far post header from Paul Merson's left wing cross but otherwise it was a day to forget. It was as well for Pompey that they won; so too did all the top six save Sheffield United, who went down at home to Norwich.

Redknapp said: "I knew it would be tough. I saw Gillingham at Reading and they impressed me. They should have beaten Leeds over two matches in the cup and beat Leicester last month. We are not going to beat teams 6-2 every week." Hessenthaler, while aggrieved with reason that Gillingham did not at least draw, said: "Portsmouth and Leicester are the best two teams in the division. They will both go up. Pompey have some fantastic players."

Portsmouth (3-4-1-2): Hislop; Primus, De Zeeuw, Festa; Harper, Sherwood, Quashie, Taylor; Merson (O'Neil 90); Yakubu (Pericard 83), Todorov.
Subs (not used): Kawaguchi, Diabate, Tavlaridis.
Goal: De Zeeuw (58).
Gillingham (4-4-2): Brown; Nosworthy, Ashby, Hope, Edge; Hessenthaler, Smith, Southall, Shaw; Wallace, Ipoua (Sidibe 66).

DERBY DAYS

Paolo Di Canio was having a spat with West Ham, so it was hardly surprising to see his name being linked with Harry Redknapp and Pompey. Di Canio was told he was not going to be offered a new contract by Redknapp's successor, Glenn Roeder, and the great man had not taken it very well. Redknapp, sensing that he might have a head start in any future bidding as the manager who took him to West Ham, wasted no time in expressing his admiration: "I'd love to have Paolo here. He's a fantastic footballer; he'd set the crowd alight. The trouble is his wages. They are way, way beyond us. We can't go out and pay ridiculous wages. But it all depends, you never know." Those wages were thought to be £40,000 a week and, in an era of declining footballer salaries, he was unlikely to be so well off again, but there was no denying that Di Canio and Redknapp had a close relationship based on mutual respect.

In the meantime, the thin line between success and failure as a manager was apparent again when two former Pompey bosses, Terry Fenwick and Neil McNab, departed on the same day having failed at Northampton and Exeter respectively. More positively, Pompey's success was being felt around the catchment area. Typical of that was the club's Football in the Community department, whose school half-term holiday coaching courses were sold out. The month ended with Pompey again top, the finishing line now within sight. It was almost dull; Leicester were clutching at Pompey's coat-tails as usual and the rest were nowhere to be seen. Roll on March.

TOP 6 AT END OF FEBRUARY 2003

	P	W	D	L	F	A	Pts
PORTSMOUTH	33	20	10	3	67	32	70
Leicester City	33	20	8	5	56	30	68
Reading	33	18	4	11	44	31	58
Sheffield United	32	16	7	9	47	35	55
Nottingham Forest	32	15	9	8	55	32	54
Wolverhampton Wdrs	33	14	10	9	56	36	52

11

ON THE BRINK

POMPEY'S INEXORABLE RISE to the Premiership continued in March with four wins, a draw and a defeat. The biggest win, 5-0 at Millwall, was achieved without a Pompey away fan in sight (officially) and the only defeat, at Wimbledon, was played out in front of 9,000 Pompey fans who outnumbered home fans by ten to one. In addition, Harry Redknapp was strongly linked with the impending managerial vacancy at Fulham, put his waterfront home up for sale at £3.25m and failed in a bid to sign the one Premiership-calibre player, Hermann Hreidarsson, who did not fall into the "getting-on-a-bit" category.

But first to Millwall, a dubious pleasure at the best of times but all the more pleasurable this year because Pompey were well on course for promotion and old and bitter rivals Millwall were languishing unremarkably in the middle of the table going nowhere. All away fans had been banned from the New Den because of their supporters' record for violence and the insatiable demand among Pompey's followers was only partially pla-

Redknapp - linked in March with Harrods, homes and Hreidarsson.

cated by the installation of a screen at Fratton Park. More diehard fans, refusing to let something as trivial as a total ban get in their way, infiltrated the Millwall support while John Westwood was treated to a seat in the directors' box where he was on his best behaviour. A young couple, choosing Fratton Park as the venue for their wedding, suddenly found their big day had been expanded by the arrival of a few thousand uninvited guests. But the potential problem was solved when Pompey fans were accommodated in the South Stand to watch the match on screen and the wedding ceremony took place with due reverence in front of the Fratton End.

Saturday, March 1

MILLWALL 0
PORTSMOUTH 5

It did not matter that Pompey fans had been barred from the New Den. Pompey were awesome. Even Millwall supporters, not known for their benevolence of heart, were forced to applaud as Pompey ran riot and Paul Merson, substituted with nine minutes remaining, even got a standing ovation. It was Pompey's biggest away win since February 10, 1973 when they won by a similar score at Preston, a result incidentally

Merson - standing ovation from the Millwall fans.

which signalled the end of the managerial reign at Deepdale of Alan Ball's father. The difference here was Millwall's lamentable defending. In terms of shots on target they actually matched Pompey; it was just that Pompey kept scoring and Millwall did not. Millwall had 17 shots, six of them on target, while Pompey had ten shots, eight on target and five of them ending in goals. Yakubu's pace caused all sorts of problems, scoring twice in a ten-minute spell, sliding home Harper's cross and then, following a Merson defence-splitter, converting Todorov's pass. Tim Sherwood headed in his first for Pompey and then Merson set up Todorov on the stroke of half-time. Millwall fans turned on their own players, although Hislop made two smart saves and Neil Harris shot over from three yards. Yakubu hit the bar and was denied a hat-trick when tripped by Paul Robinson in the area. Merson duly converted the penalty before receiving his ovation, his job done to perfection once more. "They don't do that to too many players, do they? I take it as a great honour," he said. Todorov missed a sitter in the dying minutes so that as Millwall's support hurried to the exits they knew they had got off lightly at 5-0. Wise and Quashie got into a scrape with Quashie picking up his tenth yellow card, which was to rule him out of matches against Wolves and Coventry.

With Reading losing at Wimbledon, the gap between first and third was now 15 points. Redknapp knew the significance of both results: "To come to Millwall and win 5-0 is a terrific performance, especially when they had players like Dennis Wise coming back from injury. It's hard to say whether this was our best away display of the season because we have done that all season, week in and week out. We even missed a couple of good chances but it was hard for Millwall. They kept plugging away and Shaka made two great saves." For Millwall striker and Pompey fan Steve Claridge it was a chastening experience. It was not as though the Pompey players were old mates from his time at Fratton Park. Only Harper and Quashie of the starting line-up remained from his brief spell in charge: "'Pompey will go up as champions, there's no doubt about that," he said.

Millwall (4-4-2): Warner; Reid, Robinson, Ward, Ryan; Ifill, Wise, Livermore, Kinet; Harris, Claridge (Sadlier 56).
Subs (not used): Gueret, Dunne, Hearn, Rees.
Booked: Livermore, Wise, Robinson.
Portsmouth (3-4-1-2): Hislop; Primus, De Zeeuw, Festa; Harper (Crowe 59), Sherwood, Quashie, Taylor; Merson (Diabate 81); Yakubu, Todorov (Pericard 77).
Subs (not used): Kawaguchi, O'Neil.
Goals: Yakubu (15, 25), Sherwood (31), Todorov (45), Merson (pen 72).
Booked: Quashie, Crowe.
Attendance: 9,697.
Referee: H Webb (South Yorkshire).

As Quashie was left to contemplate his two-match ban at such an important juncture in the season, Kevin Harper reckoned it didn't much matter: "Teams don't know how to stop us when we are playing at our best," he said. "We firmly believe that we have the Premiership in our sights and if we keep maintaining our standards there is nothing to fear. Against Millwall we were absolutely brilliant at times." Steve Stone, meanwhile, was winning an important battle of his own in overcoming a persistent hamstring injury. Back in the reserves in a 4-0 win over Cardiff, Stone played his first match for two months without any reaction. In the Pompey camp, all was running smoothly.

Tuesday, March 4

WIMBLEDON 2
PORTSMOUTH 1

Deprived of their Saturday at Millwall, Pompey fans made up for it in style when they swamped Selhurst Park, troubled home of Wimbledon. There was plenty of room. The controversial plan of chairman Charles Koppel to relocate the club to the virgin territory of Milton Keynes had caused massive disaffection among Dons fans. Not that there were too many of them now. They were all watching AFC Wimbledon and, in a crowd of 10,356, it was reckoned Pompey accounted for 9,000 and perhaps even more. The previous best crowd had been 6,538 for the 'visit' of landlords Crystal Palace. All other matches had failed to attract beyond 4,000 and one fixture enticed 849 away from their firesides and Teletext controls.

Gary Lineker always reckoned it was best to watch Wimbledon matches on Teletext and while they found it hard to shrug off the old route-one image, this was no longer the way the Dons now played their football, as Pompey fans would testify. Of all the teams Pompey met in this triumphant season, Wimbledon's neat, incisive football, backed by youth and pace, caused them as much trouble as any. So it proved here, even after Merson had given the travelling army plenty to cheer with his tenth of the season midway through the first half. Todorov's shot was saved by Davis, who received a night of abuse after his Fratton Park clanger, but there was room on the edge of the area for Merson to convert the rebound. Pompey lost Crowe with a foot injury after 33 minutes and, with Harper and Stone not playing, there was no

**Crowe - limped off
with foot injury.**

right-sided cover. Wimbledon sensed their chance, sent on Patrick Agyemang and Joel McAnuff as substitutes and suddenly Pompey were on the back foot. Not that they were in any mood to surrender their lead and it took 66 minutes for the Dons to draw level. Neil Shipperley, another player to catch the bile of Pompey fans for his Southampton links, headed down a Peter Hawkins cross and Agyemang drilled a shot past Hislop.

The match could have gone either way at this stage and the turning point came in the 84th minute of a keenly contested affair. Pompey were convinced Pericard had been brought down by Moritz Volz in the area but referee Peter Walton waved play on. There was still resentment in the air as Wimbledon snatched the winner three minutes from time, Nigel Reo-Coker weaving his way through a retreating defence from midfield for Gareth Ainsworth to finish from 12 yards. It was Pompey's first away defeat since September 21 at Norwich thirteen largely-glorious games ago.

Redknapp wasn't too despondent, the penalty rejection aside: "We had a nailed-on penalty five minutes from the end and as soon as it wasn't given I feared they might go down the other end and nick a goal. And they did. This defeat is not a wake-up call because we have never been asleep. Five wins from our last

eleven matches should be enough. We have got some big games coming up so we have got to keep on concentrating."

Wimbledon (4-4-2): Davis; Volz, Williams, Andersen, Hawkins; Ainsworth, Morgan (McAnuff 62), Reo-Coker, Tapp; Shipperley, Gray (Agyemang 58).
Subs (not used): Gier, Darlington, Gore.
Goals: Agyemang (66), Ainsworth (87).
Portsmouth (3-4-1-2): Hislop; Primus, De Zeeuw, Festa; Crowe (O'Neil 33), Sherwood, Quashie, Taylor; Merson; Yakubu, Todorov (Pericard 80).
Subs (not used): Kawaguchi, Tavlaridis, Diabate.
Goal: Merson (26).
Booked: Sherwood, Quashie.
Attendance: 10,356.
Referee: P Walton (Northamptonshire).

One of the more noticeable features of recent matches had been the decline from the very high standards he had set himself of Matt Taylor. The dashes down the left wing had become fewer and his involvement more peripheral. Only now was it revealed that Taylor's heel spur problem was worse than originally feared. Medical examinations had decided that an operation was required sooner or later. It was not pressing, so Taylor resolved to keep playing for a little longer, as long as he was able and as long as Pompey needed him. There was a distinct lack of cover available to Redknapp. Jamie Vincent was the obvious replacement as the only other left-back on the club's books, but he was so far out of the picture as to not exist; Claridge's £800,000 present to Pompey spent the sea-

ON THE BRINK

Festa - pressed into an emergency role as left-back.

Tavlaridis - returned to Arsenal, a useful job done.

third month on loan at Bournemouth and despatching Stathis Tavlaridis back to Arsenal's reserves, a useful job done.

son going through the motions in the reserves, uncomplaining but unwanted. Gianluca Festa, that reliable old Italian, was ultimately pressed into emergency action down the left, although Redknapp was forced to concede that Festa had never played there in 16 years of top class football. Not that the manager appeared to be concerned about lack of players, allowing Lewis Buxton to spend a

The atmosphere around Fratton Park at this time was anything but tense, not even Taylor's prolonged injury casting a cloud over Pompey's almost leisurely progress to the Premiership. Paul Merson was looking to the future when he said Pompey should be looking to challenges on the horizon: "We will need six players if we go up," the great man warned. "Make no mistake, the Premiership is a whole new ball game and we cannot go up unprepared."

SLEEPING GIANT AWAKES

Wednesday, March 12

PORTSMOUTH 3
NORWICH CITY 2

Norwich came to Fratton Park in search of a double and no other team was ever in that position. Sky TV were in their familiar position above the South Stand and their viewers were in for a treat. Five goals, goalmouth action at both ends and in the end Pompey's superior goal-scoring power was the telling factor. Pompey did their best to throw it away, twice allowing Norwich to equalise and then hanging on grimly at the end as Norwich, battling for play-off points, threw everyone forward in a bid to salvage a draw from a match they might easily have won. Pompey did not manage a shot until the 36th minute and it needed an injury to Harper, suffering a recurrence to a calf muscle, to breathe life into them, ironically.

Switching to 4-3-1-2, Pompey were more at ease with them-selves after the break and Todorov put in Yakubu for their first after 57 minutes. It was the Nigerian's sixth goal in seven

**Festa, Sherwood and Primus in the thick
of the action against Norwich's Gary Holt.**

games and was the signal for a hectic spell in which the sides swapped goals with merry abandon. Within 60 seconds Norwich were level. Celebrating Pompey fans were silenced when Mark Rivers got behind the labouring Taylor for Clint Easton to score from close range. Almost immediately Pompey were ahead again, former Canary Sherwood supplying the pass for Yakubu to set up Todorov. Still Norwich were not beaten and three minutes later Zema Abbey's cross caused chaos in the defence and Rivers blasted in from the edge of the area. At 2-2, anything could have happened and in the end it needed a mistake by goalkeeper Robert Green, who made a hash of Merson's corner by punching against one of his own players, for Pompey to grab a winner. The ever-ruthless Todorov snapped up the rebound, but even then Norwich refused to concede defeat and it needed a high class save from Hislop to keep out a stoppage time shot from Abbey when a third equaliser seemed inevitable. Hislop was not overly-extended during the season but his Premiership ability was always evident when it was needed, as it was here.

Redknapp admitted Norwich had played well and had cause to feel they had deserved some reward from a turbulent match in which they probably enjoyed the greater share of possession:

"The first half was probably as bad as we have played all season. We simply never gave up, that's what we're like. It would be hard to throw it all away now. Sheffield United are the only team who can do anything. Norwich were a whisker away from the Premiership last season so we were never going to murder them. We had to be patient, mind you. Jim Smith was getting a bit excited on the bench next to me. The team was thrown together. Paul Merson was not 100 per cent because of 'flu. Kevin Harper had not trained properly. We are the leading scorers in the league and even when we are not playing well we always think we can get a goal or two."

Portsmouth (3-4-1-2): Hislop; Primus, Festa, De Zeeuw; Harper (O'Neil 45), Sherwood, Quashie (Diabate 66), Taylor; Merson (Foxe 74); Yakubu, Todorov.
Subs (not used): Kawaguchi, Pericard.
Goals: Yakubu (57), Todorov (59, 72).
Booked: Primus.
Norwich (4-4-2): Green; Nedergaard (Roberts 88), Mackay, Bromby, Drury; Rivers, Holt, Russell (Emblen 88), Easton; Abbey, McVeigh (Nielsen 79).
Subs (not used): Crichton, Shackell.
Goals: Easton (58), Rivers (62).
Booked: Holt.
Attendance: 19,221.
Referee: D Gallagher (Oxfordshire).

It didn't escape notice that Gordon Strachan and Glenn Hoddle had watched the Norwich match and perhaps Yakubu was not the only target. It was assumed he was but Hoddle was almost certainly checking the progress of Matt Taylor. Spurs were to keen to sign him the previous summer but Redknapp took advantage of their sloth and now he had become one of the best left wing-backs outside the Premiership. Taylor, with an operation looming, was not at his best against Norwich but it was hard to play down the fantastic contribution he had made to Pompey's season overall, something Hoddle was bound to have recognised.

Todorov's goals, meanwhile, had got him back into the Bulgarian squad on a regular basis and when he, Yakubu, Diabate and Kawaguchi were called into their national sides, Pompey were able to call off their match with Burnley which had been scheduled for Fratton Park on March 29. For Kawaguchi, not first choice for club or country, it was a chance to impress Japan's new coach, the Brazilian superstar Zico. Keen to bolster Pompey's income in a way that did not necessarily require his own input, Mandaric offered a 'present' to loyal fans who purchased a season ticket for next year now. Irrespective of which division Pompey might be in - and Premiership football beckoned - this was at the same price they were paying already. A bargain indeed and a market ploy calculated to bring in enough cash to help Redknapp in the summer ahead.

Kawaguchi - keen to impress Japan's new coach, the great Brazilian Zico.

Saturday, March 15

**PORTSMOUTH 1
WOLVES 0**

Wolves had not been able to mount the expected challenge to Pompey or Leicester and they came to Fratton Park, as Norwich had done a few days earlier, with the play-offs as their only achievable prospect. Wolves had shown their capability in the FA Cup, defeating Newcastle and Leicester before going down to Southampton in the quarter-finals but, overall, Dave Jones's team had not put together a decent run in the league. Until now. They arrived with a record of six matches unbeaten, including successive away wins at Ipswich, Preston and Reading. Taylor at last gave way to his injury and prepared for his operation knowing that his next likely action would be in the Premiership, providing his team-mates did not falter in his absence. At least Steve Stone was fit again while O'Neil took over from the suspended Quashie.

It should have been a great match with so much depending on it but, as a spectacle, it was poor. Jones had lost three of his regular back four overnight to illness and injury and there was some defensive confusion as Stone strode through from mid-field unchallenged to beat Matt Murray. Mark Clyde should have equalised but shot over from 12 yards, but it was a rare incident in a match largely devoid of excitement or quality. Credit the Pompey defence, they gave Kenny Miller little room to add to his 20 goals while, at the other end, once Wolves had got them-selves organised, it was just as sterile. Pompey's defenders - De Zeeuw, Primus, Foxe and Festa - gave little away over the season and were always reliable when they needed to be. Primus, though not a Redknapp signing, and De Zeeuw, came from Reading and Wigan respectively.

Steve Stone salutes the Milton End after his winning goal against Wolves.

Foxe was in West Ham's reserves and Middlesbrough did not think Festa had another season in him at the top level. Yet all of them were as important to Pompey as Todorov's goals at the other end.

In truth, Wolves never looked likely to level once they had gone behind. Redknapp chose Festa as his man of the match: "Festa has never played at left back in his life. But he was willing to try it and did a great job. It was a tight game and Wolves have many players who cost a lot compared with my squad. We are never going to get a better chance than this and if we don't get promoted I won't be able to show my face around here again." Jones, beaten twice in Hampshire in less than a week, allayed Redknapp's fears: "I think Portsmouth will win promotion but whether they can stay in the Premiership, I don't know. We have produced two good performances against them, matching them all the way, but we have only one point to show for it."

Festa would continue to play down the left side, according to Redknapp, for the foreseeable future, possibly the rest of the season - and the durable Festa was not complaining. The future of the explosive Yakubu occupied the manager's attention. Pompey had first refusal on him with Maccabi Haifa but the Israelis knew he would be in demand once exposed to English football and they were not budging from their £4m valuation. Redknapp said: "Yakubu has done tremendously well since he came over here. He looks a tremendous prospect at 20 and I just wonder whether we will be able to buy him."

Merson was taking a more immediate view of life at Fratton Park: "Three more wins will do us," he said. The way prospective rivals were falling away, it was hard to disagree with his verdict, nor was it difficult to understand Redknapp's desire to look beyond the season in progress. Matches were coming thick and fast now and, after two shaky but successful home wins, Pompey were on their travels again, this time to Highfield Road. Pompey were getting far better results away than at Fratton Park - and so it proved again.

Portsmouth (4-3-1-2): Hislop; Primus (Harper 45), Foxe, De Zeeuw, Festa; Stone, Sherwood, O'Neil; Merson; Yakubu (Diabate 90), Todorov (Burton 80).
Subs (not used): Kawaguchi, Pericard.
Goal: Stone (4).
Booked: Stone, Foxe.
Wolves (4-4-2): Murray; Edworthy, Clyde, Pollet, Irwin; Rae, Ince, Cameron (Newton 45), Kennedy; Sturridge, Miller (Proudlock 83).
Subs (not used): Oakes, Cooper, Naylor.
Booked: Cameron, Ince, Rae.
Attendance: 19,558.
Referee: P Dowd (Staffordshire).

Right: Yakubu - a tremendous prospect at only 20.

SLEEPING GIANT AWAKES

Wednesday, March 19

COVENTRY CITY 0
PORTSMOUTH 4

Pompey's record at Coventry did not bear close scrutiny. Lanky striker Ray Hiron, now working in leisure at the Mountbatten Sports Centre in Portsmouth, scored the club's last goal there on the last day of 1966. But today Pompey found Coventry in the middle of a lean spell. They had not won at home since Boxing Day and had drifted from play-off contention into the bottom half of the table, winning at Grimsby as their only success anywhere in 13 matches.

There was just a little bit of pressure on Pompey in that Sheffield United and Leicester had won the previous day, but any nerves were quickly banished. Within 23 minutes, Pompey were 3-0 up with another rapid and clinical display of finishing. Coventry almost scored through Dean Holdsworth but, in a typically incisive counter-attack, Todorov hit a post and Gary Caldwell turned the ball over his own line. Calum Davenport, who had been dispossessed for the first goal, was caught again by Yakubu whose pass to O'Neil allowed Stone to score. "Goodbye to the Nationwide", chanted Pompey fans six minutes later when Yakubu outpaced Pead down the left for

Harper to score again. Strange as it may seem, Coventry had more shots on target than Pompey but Hislop made three outstanding saves from Holdsworth, Joachim and Eustace and, when it came to finishing, Pompey were on their own. Even the loss of De Zeeuw after 25 minutes with an ankle injury failed to disrupt Pompey, the Finnish international Markus Heikkinen slotting in perfectly at the heart of the defence.

Hislop - made three outstanding saves.

Harper - on target again at Coventry.

moment with our passing and counter-attacking. It shows our confidence if I'm scoring with my left foot."

Redknapp, joyous on the pitch at the end, made no attempt to hide his pleasure at the scoreline: "Looking at their midfield four I thought it was going to be a tough game. But it wasn't. To score four goals away from home is a great performance. You always want perfection. At half-time I still thought we could do better. Every team has a blip but we have been consistent right through. On paper, we had three tough match-es against Norwich, Wolves and Coventry and we won them all. At the start of the season I did not expect to finish above any of them."

Coventry (4-4-2): Hyldgaard; Pead, Shaw, Davenport, Caldwell; Eustace, McAllister, Chippo (Whing 85), Safri (McSheffrey 66); Holdsworth, Joachim.
Subs (not used): Debec, Jansen, Engonga.
Portsmouth (3-4-1-2): Hislop; Foxe, De Zeeuw (Heikkinen 25), Festa; Stone (Diabate 75), Sherwood, O'Neil, Harper; Merson; Yakubu, Todorov (Pericard 68).
Subs (not used): Kawaguchi, Burton.
Goals: Caldwell (o.g. 14), Stone (17), Harper (23), Merson (68).
Booked: Sherwood.
Attendance: 13,922.
Referee: M Ryan (Lancashire).

Much as Coventry pressed for-ward in search of a consolation, Pompey looked capable of scoring again and, after Stone and Todorov had combined, Merson celebrated the imminence of his 35th birthday by firing home with his little-used left foot. Merson said: "I think I should be awarded two goals for every one I score with my left foot because it does not happen very often. I have scored 150 goals in my career but not too many with my left. We're just killing off teams at the

Pompey's youth squad, in the hands at various levels of Dave Hurst, Shaun North and Mark O'Connor, had in Gary O'Neil a shining example of what could be achieved by spotting and developing teenage talent. O'Neil was now worth a sizeable figure

Gary O'Neil - a shining example of what could be achieved with a youth development programme.

in the transfer market, if ever Pompey chose to sell him, and there were a few others bubbling under the first team squad. Shaun Cooper, Lewis Buxton and Rowan Vine, on loan at Brentford, were prospects for the future but, as the Premiership neared with every day, the stakes were being raised. Pompey's youth development programme was now charged, not with finding players capable of playing league football, but capable of playing in the Premiership. It was and remains a tall order. When Redknapp first became manager he expressed surprise that a working class city like Portsmouth had not produced a steady stream of young talent. But a look at the record books reveals that Portsmouth has never been a prolific breeding ground for footballers. Supporters of an older generation will recall a former manager, George Smith, in the early 1960s abandoning the costly youth setup with a dismissive comment that earned notoriety: "There are only fish in the sea around Portsmouth." While the occasional Ports-mouth-born player has since emerged at lower levels, in the main he has been vindicated. Only Steve Foster in the intervening 40 or more years has gone on to play for England and even O'Neil is originally from south London.

But, in youth terms, hope springs eternal and in March it was announced that three young players were stepping up to become full professionals. Chris Clark, a young striker, went one stage further by being named as a substitute in the next match at Preston. Terry Parker and Anthony Pulis were the others. Pulis might have followed his father, Tony, to Stoke but he chose to stay on and for all of them the incentive of playing at Old Trafford and Highbury is the stuff of dreams for less fortunate contemporaries.

Saturday, March 22

PRESTON NORTH END 1 PORTSMOUTH 1

It was a match which marked Harry Redknapp's year in charge. It had been a momentous year as the manager conceded in the aftermath of a satisfactory draw: "It's been incredible. I came here at the back end of last season and my first game was at Preston. I didn't have much of a season and I didn't fancy the job, to be honest with you. Even after I took it I was asking myself why. But the lads have been fantastic. They have all worked their socks off; we have scored lots of goals and won lots of matches. We have lost four games all season so it's been an incredible turnaround. I have loved every minute of it and working alongside Jim Smith has been an experience in itself."

So much for reflection. Preston had won four of their last five matches and survived a first half battering to snatch a late equaliser. For once, the Pompey goal machine failed to function properly. Primus returned to the defence and O'Neil retained his place in midfield, allowing Clark to sit on the bench for the first time. Stone and Harper combined for Yakubu to open the scoring in the fifth minute and another Pompey supershow looked about to be unfurled. But, as Pompey searched for their eleventh away win, Todorov, O'Neil and Merson either missed or were denied by David Lucas. Preston improved after the break but they had to wait until the 89th minute before levelling when, from a free-kick, Paul McKenna conjured a goal from 25 yards. It could even have been worse for Pompey in the dying seconds when Tyrone Mears and Simon Lynch went desperately close to a Preston winner.

Redknapp thought the free-kick which led to McKenna's goal was harshly given: "I could not see Preston getting a goal," he said. "We are never negative when we go away from home and we try to win every game. At Bournemouth I took them up with two tiny wingers with 97 points. I want my teams to play football and I will never encourage them to lump the ball forward. It's just not the way I play. Preston were a good side last season and Craig Brown has been unlucky to lose Ricardo Fuller with injury but we should have beaten them."

Preston (4-4-2): Lucas; Alexander, Lucketti, Broomes (O'Neil 87), Edwards; Cartwright (Mears 79), Etuhu, McKenna, Lewis; Koumantarakis (Lynch 55), Cresswell.
Subs (not used): Skora, Lonergan.
Goal: McKenna (89).
Portsmouth (3-4-1-2): Hislop; Primus, Foxe, Festa; Stone, Sherwood, O'Neil, Harper; Merson; Todorov (Burton 79), Yakubu.
Subs (not used): Kawaguchi, Diabate, Heikkinen, Clark.
Goal: Yakubu (5).
Attendance: 16,665.
Referee: M Messias (North Yorkshire).

This was Pompey's last match in March but time was not wasted. Redknapp travelled to Spain to watch Real Betis against Malaga with next season very much in mind. Romanian defender Iulian Filipescu, 29, and Malaga's Uruguyan striker Dario Silva, 30, impressed the Pompey manager but rumours abounded that his real target was the £22m Brazilian star Denilson, a Betis substitute. Chief scout Stuart Morgan went to Germany to view Hertha Berlin pair Josip Simunic, a Croatian international defender, and German Stefan Bienlich. Coach Kevin Bond ran the rule over known Pompey target, Stijn Vreven. The hunt was on.

The transfer deadline came ever closer and for a time it looked as if Pompey, despite the manager's protestations, might be involved. The centre of the intrigue was Hreidarsson, a 28-year old Icelandic international, at Ipswich. Ipswich wanted to keep him but not his wages and the club's administrators made it clear he had to go. Hreidarsson was believed to be earning £17,000 a week and Redknapp sensed the chance to do with him and Ipswich what he had done so successfully with Merson, Sherwood and Stone, namely paying a chunk of his wages and get the selling club to provide the rest via a pay-off. Hreidarsson even got as far as opening talks with Pompey but

Harry Redknapp - pictured in his Bournemouth days, Rothmans
at the ready to help his search for two tiny wingers.

he was reluctant to uproot his family from the Suffolk country-side and drop down a division, even if only temporarily. Charlton entered the fray late in the day, told him he could continue to live in Suffolk and agreed to take him on even though he was injured. Hreidarsson told Pompey he was sorry not to be joining them and wished them well but the fact that Charlton were an established Premiership side, not one with aspirations to reach that level, helped him choose all the more easily. The eventual fee was around £900,000. Pompey were duly linked with Newcastle's Greek defender Nikos Dabizas and Redknapp later flew to watch Croatia versus Belgium, renewing interest in 24-year-old goalkeeper Stipe Pletikosa, but the manager was at pains to point out that the squad which had earned promotion would be given every opportunity to prove they could play in the Premiership.

Redknapp, meanwhile, was one of the early front-runners (in the newspapers at least) to take over from departing boss Jean Tigana at Fulham but Harry did not let the rumours grow and multiply. There was no interest from Fulham in him, he said, and no interest by him in Fulham. End of story. Harry's palatial seaside home overlooking Poole Harbour was now on the market, perhaps fuelling that Fulham speculation, at a cool £3.25m. But he was not going far. He had his

eyes on another not far away with its own gatehouse in which he hoped to install his father, a former fish and chip shop owner in the East End. But Harry Snr was reluctant to leave his roots and friends. Property was obviously on the manager's mind when he warned that Pompey would not survive long in the Premiership unless they built a new stadium. Fratton Park had had its day. He added: "You have got to get 30,000 through the turnstiles for every game to give yourself the chance of getting in a few decent players. Look at Southampton. They've built a new stadium and have gone on to another level. We could match them. We'd get 30,000 a week easily." Looking at Southampton as an example was not something Pompey fans liked doing, but they knew he was right.

TOP 6 AT END OF MARCH 2003

	P	W	D	L	F	A	Pts
PORTSMOUTH	39	24	11	4	82	37	83
Leicester City	39	23	11	5	64	35	80
Sheffield United	38	20	9	9	61	41	69
Reading	39	21	4	14	49	38	67
Nottingham Forest	38	18	11	9	69	37	65
Wolverhampton Wdrs	39	17	12	10	68	38	63

12

CHAMPIONS

Jim Smith, Harry Redknapp and Kevin Bond, in their differing ways, keep a watchful eye on a training ground routine.

SPRING APPROACHED AND SO too did the last lap of a long, long season. April has a habit of making fools out of football teams; remember Wolves the same time last year. Pompey entered the last full month in top-class condition, the pack of clubs trailing behind, all failing to keep up with the pace set by Redknapp's squad in much the same way Paula Radcliffe had decimated her opposition in winning the London Marathon, also in this same crucial month. There were some tough matches ahead, of that there was no doubt, but the feeling at Fratton Park was that it would need a collapse of Devon Loch proportions for Pompey to fail. And so to the Midlands, to Walsall's Bescot Stadium, for just the sort of match champions-elect must be expected to win. Walsall were on the relegation fringes and in exactly the sort of position Pompey normally found themselves in at this stage of the season. Not this season, though.

Saturday, April 5

**WALSALL 1
PORTSMOUTH 2**

Pompey needed no reminder that Colin Lee's beleaguered team had proved unexpectedly difficult opposition when the teams met at Fratton Park in November. There was an evening kick-off and extra pressure was applied by Leicester's defeat of Grimsby earlier in the day, so Pompey could not afford to slip up if they wanted to stay top. With Quashie back, everything went according to plan for 45 minutes, apart from a hamstring injury which forced Yakubu to leave the field. Kevin Harper, who once spent three months on loan at Walsall when at Derby, sprinted half the length of the field to collect Stone's pass and beat Ward with a curling shot. When Todorov headed in Sherwood's cross, a repeat of Millwall or Coventry looked a distinct possibility as Pompey passed the ball around at will.

Kevin Harper - sprinted half the length of the field to score.

But on the stroke of half time, Foxe was caught in possession and Junior punished him further by going on to score. It was a different, more evenly-contested second half and wayward shooting by Darren Wrack and Jorge Leitao spared Pompey blushes. There was also a scare when Hislop appeared to handle outside the area but Pompey held on for their eleventh away win less comfortably than had earlier seemed probable.

Redknapp knew Hislop had been lucky: "I have never seen him punch a ball before and after that I never want to see it again." As to the rest of the performance, Redknapp praised Todorov, who he believed was one of the few Pompey players to respond consistently over the 90 minutes: "Toddy was outstanding all night. Two goals up, I was looking forward to sitting back and enjoying the match but Hayden Foxe took a liberty and got punished and that changed the whole game. Foxey is a premier league player. It's like Rio Ferdinand at Manchester United. Sometimes he can get caught out but if you want players who just kick the ball up in the air then Rio and Foxey are not your men."

Walsall (4-4-2): Ward; Bazeley, Roper, Carbon, Aranalde; Sonner, Samways, Corica (Hay 63), Wrack (Matias 88); Junior, Leitao (Zdrilic 83).
Subs (not used): Harris, Barras.
Goal: Junior (45).
Portsmouth (3-4-1-2): Hislop; Primus, Foxe, Festa; Stone, Sherwood, Quashie, Harper; Merson (O'Neil 89); Todorov, Yakubu (Burton 24).
Subs (not used): Kawaguchi, Heikkinen, Diabate.
Booked: Merson.
Goals: Harper (15), Todorov (33).
Attendance: 7,899.
Referee: S Mathieson (Cheshire).

As Pompey neared their goal of Premiership football, the nation was at war. The aircraft carrier Ark Royal had left Portsmouth Harbour in a flurry of publicity and to tumultuous cheering from the shore. There were plenty of Pompey fans serving aboard Ark Royal and Redknapp dedicated the Walsall victory to them at a time when British forces were sustaining casualties on their march through Iraq. Match videos were sent to the crew with a good-luck message, although the Sky TV coverage would have been watched live in the Gulf by off-duty sailors. They would have noted the Pompey support, as had Mandaric: "Words can't express my admiration for these people. Even in times such as these they can't remain divorced from their football team and are still cheering them on. We truly have the best supporters in the country."

As a precaution, Lee Bradbury was brought back from his loan spell at Sheffield Wednesday and was lined up to face his old club immediately, while the fans Mandaric so raved about braved freezing temperatures to camp out all night to be certain they had tickets for Pompey's last match of the season at Bradford City. Only 6,491 were available and Ian Blackmore, 45, of Southsea had arrived eleven hours before the ticket office opened at 8am to be sure of his prize: "I had to be first in the queue or I would have had eleven mates who would have strung me up. We've waited 25 years for a day like this and I didn't want to miss it." Tickets soon went. Jason Crowe was offered a new one-year contract and Roma's Ivory Coast international defender Saliou Lassissi was lined up for a trial on the recommendation of Diabate, an international

Play up Pompey! - fans' expectations were high for the visit of Sheffield Wednesday.

teammate. The only drawback was a lack of match fitness.

Saturday, April 12

PORTSMOUTH 1
SHEFFIELD WEDNESDAY 2

Oh dear. Pompey went into the match needing three points to guarantee promotion and a sell-out Fratton Park was tingling with expectation. After all, this was top versus bottom and surely nothing could go wrong at this late stage? The mood was distinctly triumphalist, the banners were at the ready, the ticker-tape was stored in carrier bags and all that was needed was for Pompey to show up, knock off the opposition as they had done all season and the celebrations could begin.

But with Yakubu initially ruled out for the season by a hamstring injury and Pericard also missing, Pompey had to call up Bradbury seven days after he had been playing for Wednesday. It was his first Pompey start for 16 months and, within 20 minutes, he was on the scoresheet, swivelling sharply to take advantage of Kevin Pressman's failure to hold a Todorov shot. The Pompey faithful sat back waiting for Wednesday to capitulate as so many others had done before them but Stone shot into the side netting, Bradbury was denied by Pressman and Merson shot over. The annihilation never

CHAMPIONS

The perfect return - Lee Bradbury celebrates the opening goal.

happened as Wednesday grew stronger at set-pieces and started to play on the nervousness of Pompey players and their supporters. Pompey were 14 minutes from the Premiership when Linvoy Primus, man of the season, sliced a clearance into the path of Ashley Westwood, who shuffled home a scrappy and unsatisfactory equaliser.

The match was heading for a draw when Wednesday scored the winner in injury time, a highly controversial affair in which Pompey claimed goalscorer Michael Reddy was not ten yards away when Gianluca Festa attempted a quick free-kick. Reddy still had a lot to do but

raced from the halfway line before beating Hislop. Fratton Park was silent, save for the 1,000 travelling away fans. Worse still, Leicester were now top of the table, a position held by Pompey uninterrupted since August. At the end there were delirious scenes of embracing players and officials on the pitch. But they were not from Portsmouth.

Redknapp put it in perspective when he said: "It's a disappointment for the fans but they don't see us lose very often. Everyone thought it would be singing and dancing but Sheffield Wednesday are fighting for their lives." Instead, Redknapp reserved his

**Party poopers - Wednesday celebrate their victory
as shocked Pompey fans look on.**

ire for referee David Crick for the confusion over the free-kick from which the winner had emanated: "I have never seen anything like it. I don't mind losing, but not like that. It was the most scandalous goal I have ever seen in football. I spoke to the referee afterwards and I don't think he understood what he had done." Betraying his own jitters, perhaps, Redknapp turned on a reporter who had asked him if he had considered bringing on Gary O'Neil. Offering to swap jobs with the reporter, Harry stormed off in a hail of expletives. The party was definitely delayed.

Portsmouth (3-4-1-2): Hislop; Primus, Foxe, Festa; Stone, Sherwood, Quashie, Harper (De Zeeuw 45); Merson; Todorov, Bradbury.
Subs (not used): Kawaguchi, O'Neil, Diabate, Burton.
Goal: Bradbury (20).
Booked: Stone, Primus.
Sheffield Wednesday (3-5-2): Pressman; Bromby, Smith, Maddix; Westwood, McLaren, Haslam, Quinn, Barry-Murphy; Owusu (Reddy 73), Kuqi (Holt 73).
Subs (not used): Stringer, Richard Evans, Wood.
Goals: Westwood (76), Reddy (90).
Booked: Maddix.
Attendance: 19,524.
Referee: D Crick (Surrey).

Pompey announced that former player-manager Steve Claridge had been awarded a benefit to be staged at Fratton Park on May 5. An International XI was to play Pompey as part of the deal which enabled Claridge to leave Wolves for Pompey years before. Claridge admitted later how delighted he had been by Pompey's promotion and was even, as he put it, "glad" for the chairman, the same chairman who had fired him after 22 matches in charge. Claridge, Titchfield-based, had been allowed to get over his hurt in an extended spell at Millwall and near the end of the season it was revealed that he had given Weymouth, where he spent three years after being sold by a Bournemouth manager by the name of Redknapp, £10,000 of his own money as part of a takeover. Much-travelled Claridge quipped: "If I gave all my old clubs £10,000 each I would be broke."

Would the Pompey faithful's expectations be thwarted again against Burnley?

Tuesday, April 15

**PORTSMOUTH 1
BURNLEY 0**

The party was back on and back on with a vengeance. The date, the time, the place will be forever part of Pompey folklore and the event, promotion to the Premiership for the first time, will be remembered by Pompey fans of all generations. Even those who saw Harris, Dickinson, Phillips and Reid in their prime were moved to a tear or two.

Steve Claridge - awarded a benefit and "glad" for the chairman.

The match itself was a tetchy, dull affair. Burnley, who twice let in seven goals at home, looked short of confidence and ideas but the longer the match went on and the longer they survived Pompey's erratic pressure, the more likely it seemed that Pompey would be thwarted yet again. Michopoulos in the Burnley goal made some great interceptions and the importance of the occasion even got to Merson, who slammed a tenth minute penalty against the underside of the bar. Bradbury and Quashie missed wonderful opportunities and Steve Davis cleared Todorov's shot from the line. Suddenly, defence-minded Burnley got forward and Gareth Taylor shot across the face of the goal while Ian Moore appeared to be brought down. The turning point was the arrival of substitute Pericard, the big striker Pompey had once feared would not play again this season. Within three minutes Pompey had got the winner, Quashie's shot finding its way across goal for unmarked Todorov to get in a shot which even then the goalkeeper got his hands to, only for the ball to cross the line. Fratton Park went wild and there was no way back for moderate Burnley.

Todorov wheels away after his shot had been willed over the line by the crowd.

CHAMPIONS

**Vincent Pericard lets the fans know the
direction Pompey are going.**

The last 17 minutes simply flew by as Pompey, their confidence restored, counted down the seconds to the final whistle - and that coveted place in the top grade. Todorov, who had been booked for celebrating his goal among fans at the Fratton End, had become the first Pompey player to reach 20 in a season since 'Corporal Punishment' himself, Guy Whittingham. But who cared who got the goal. Pompey were in the promised land and, when referee Brian Curson blew for the last time, Merson sank to the floor in relief and elation. Fans poured on to the pitch, the players were taken shoulder-high on a chaotic lap of honour and Redknapp made his way to the Fratton End to make a personal gesture of thanks to the club's hardcore support. Mandaric hugged well-wishers and waved. The place was bedlam. Television crews mingled desperately with fans on the pitch in a bid to locate Redknapp and his swamped players; high in the stands, radio reporters gabbled their joy in a torrent of words.

Redknapp later emerged from a scrum of happiness to say: "The last six minutes were the longest of my life but the players deserve it and the fans deserve it. You can see what it means to the people of Portsmouth by their

Unparalleled scenes of jubilation followed
the defeat of Burnley.

reactions. It's just fantastic. The most important thing is the team spirit. You can have the best players in the world but if there is no team spirit it means nothing. It's great for Toddy. He's got 20 goals now but got a bit of grief when he first came down. He's shown them what he can do. Where else do you find supporters like these?" Mandaric paused from his celebrations to endorse Redknapp's opinions of the Fratton faithful: "When I came to the club I told them to stick with me and I'll get you where you deserve. This is their night."

Portsmouth (3-4-1-2): Hislop; Primus, Foxe, De Zeeuw; Stone, Sherwood, Quashie, Festa; Merson, Todorov, Bradbury (Pericard 70).
Subs (not used): Kawaguchi, Harper, O'Neil, Diabate.
Goal: Todorov (73).
Booked: Festa, Todorov.
Burnley (4-4-2): Michopoulos; West, S Davis, McGregor, Gnohere (Chaplow 82); Weller, Papadopoulos (Maylett 8, O'Neill 53), Blake, Branch; I Moore, Taylor.
Subs (not used): Armstrong, Pilkington.
Booked: S Davis.
Attendance: 19,221.
Referee: B Curson (Leicestershire).

The party over, there were hangovers all over Portsmouth as workers either delayed their trek into work or did not appear at all. For Redknapp and Mandaric it was business as usual. The big question concerned the chairman, who had played coy about his future all season. Would he stay now that promotion had been achieved, or head home to California, mission accomplished? The answer was one all Pompey fans had hoped for: "Yes, I'm staying." Mandaric had told his family he had decided to delay his retirement and was preparing instead for a series of 12-hour shuttles from his west coast home to Pompey to take the club he had grown to love forward into the Premiership. He said: "It's great to be chairman of a Premiership club and I want to stay because there are improvements to be made. I want to establish this club in the top flight and to complete the stadium project. It would break my heart to leave now. I can't do it."

But there was a sting in the tail. Mandaric was only too well aware of the financial burden placed on his broad shoulders and he could not be expected to bear it alone and forever. "I am looking for investors to join me in the boardroom," he said. Sharing burdens usually means sharing power. Harry Redknapp, fresh from walking his dogs on the beach near his home, had also been reflecting on the awesome challenge ahead: "If I think too much about next season I get scared stiff. When you look at the quality of players West Ham have, it makes you realise what hard work we have ahead of us. It scares me that West Ham have struggled." There were congratulations from along the coast at St Mary's. Southampton chairman Rupert Lowe and Gordon Strachan looked forward to next season's derby matches and said Pompey's promotion was good for football on the south coast. No doubt Pompey fans were just as enthusiastic about Saints reaching the FA Cup final. There was talk of a Pompey approach for ex-Saint Iain Dowie, now manager at Oldham, with Jim Smith 'going upstairs', but Fratton Park was a mass of rumours after that Burnley match, even more than usual.

Friday, April 18

IPSWICH TOWN 3
PORTSMOUTH 0

Brought forward for television purposes, this match was a day or two too early for battle-weary Pompey. A win would have taken them five points clear of second-placed Leicester but it never looked likely to happen as the Tractor Boys, desperate for play-off points, surged into a three-goal lead within half an hour. Ipswich were perhaps the best team to visit Fratton Park and their quality was much in evidence as Martijn Reuser, Tommy Miller and Pablo Counago over-ran a tired and mistake-ridden defence to score the goals which put the match quickly out of Pompey's reach. "Three-nil to the Nationwide" sang the Ipswich fans with more than a hint of irony. They still saw themselves as a Premiership club and Pompey as, well, not.

It was the first time Pompey had failed to score in 21 league matches but the fact that Pompey had, for once, been over-run failed to deter the intrepid John Westwood. Clambering on to the roof of the hospitality boxes, bugle and bell in hand, he gave fulsome renditions of "Harry and Jim". The Harry part of the terrace song was equally fulsome in his praise of Ipswich, who, he thought, would be a major danger before the season started: "They have got quality players all over the park. I can't be too critical and we have to be very proud of what we have achieved. I'm not going to get down on the players after one defeat. Ipswich have got a forward in Marcus Bent who cost more than my whole team put together."

Ipswich (4-4-2): Marshall; Wilnis, Gaardsoe, Makin, Richards; Miller, Magilton (Wright 69), Holland, Reuser (Westlake 82); Counago, M Bent (Armstrong 82).
Subs (not used): Bowditch, Pullen.
Goals: Reuser (11), Miller (27), Counago (30).
Booked: Gaardsoe.
Portsmouth (3-4-1-2): Hislop; Primus, Foxe, De Zeeuw (O'Neil 68); Stone, Sherwood, Quashie, Festa; Merson (Harper 68); Todorov, Bradbury (Pericard 60).
Subs (not used): Kawaguchi, Diabate.
Booked: Festa, Sherwood.
Attendance: 29,396.
Referee: E Wolstenholme (Lancashire).

Gianluca Festa had been a tremendous signing, doing everything required of him, but it was clear that he was nearing the end of his career in England and Festa needed no one to tell

CHAMPIONS

Gianluca Festa - announced his return to Italy.

him. "It looks like we are going to lose him," admitted Redknapp. "His family want to go home to Italy. He's been fantastic for me, always giving 100 per cent. It'll be a big loss to see him go." But, while Festa was considering the end of his Pompey career, Redknapp was looking to strengthen for next season. Patrik Berger of Liverpool was a free agent in the summer and, no longer required at Anfield, was examining his options. Germany called but he liked the sound of the challenge at Pompey and remained top of Redknapp's list as the season drew to a close.

Meanwhile, the rich pickings at Upton Park in the wake of a possible relegation led Redknapp to be linked with several prominent Hammers' players, not least Joe Cole at the little matter of £10m. Redknapp, with the stricken Glenn Roeder in mind, promised no poaching of West Ham players in the close season, though Di Canio remained enticingly available. But all this talk of ten million pound signings was made laughable when Redknapp revealed that his players had not been able to get into their training ground the day after being promoted because landlords

Southampton University had locked the gates for Easter. It was a fact that Pompey trained at a ground nearer to Southampton city centre than Saints did, out in the New Forest at Staplewood. As Redknapp remarked, even then the pitches at the university ground were as bad as Hackney Marshes.

Monday, April 21

**PORTSMOUTH 3
READING 0**

Promotion achieved, the battle now was for the championship. Leicester had gone top on Easter Saturday but at lunchtime on Easter Monday had lost in injury time to Sheffield United. This left Pompey needing to beat the Royals to regain pole position. Reading needed to win to maintain their praiseworthy push for the play-offs the year after being promoted from the second division. So a top class match was in prospect. Much to the annoyance and bafflement of the 2,000 travelling Royals fans, it did not happen that way. Reading froze and, it's fair to say, produced a performance as poor as any seen from a visiting side at Fratton Park all season. Reading had plenty of possession but did nothing with it and Pompey, without ever being at their best, tore them apart. Pericard, restored to the starting line up,

scored twice and Todorov got the other, running from inside his own half, as Reading collapsed. Their only consolation was that other results left them needing only one point from their remaining three matches and they soon got it. But for rampant Pompey it was back to the top of the table in a welter of goals.

At the double - Vincent Pericard, with a brace against Reading, is congratulated by his teammates.

Redknapp admitted the Sheffield United win over Leicester had given him and his players a big boost: "We want to be champions," he said. Praise was reserved for Pericard and Todorov and the 92 points now achieved was a club record. As for Reading, manager Alan

Pardew congratulated Pompey but admitted: "We made it very easy for them."

Portsmouth (3-4-1-2): Hislop; Primus, Foxe, Festa; Stone, Sherwood, Quashie (O'Neil 90), Harper (De Zeeuw 85); Merson (Diabate 88); Todorov, Pericard.
Subs (not used): Kawaguchi, Burton.
Goals: Pericard (19,45), Todorov (71).
Reading (4-5-1): Hahnemann; Murty, Williams, Brown (Mackie 16), Shorey; Chadwick (Henderson 57), Hughes (Salako 76), Newman, Harper, Little; Forster.
Subs (not used): Ashdown, Cureton.
Booked: Hahnemann.
Attendance: 19,535.
Referee: G Cain (Merseyside).

Berger's pay demands were causing Pompey to think again about pursuing a player who had not made a league start all season. Take a cut, and we might be able to talk business, said Redknapp. "I like Berger," he said. "He's a Premiership-class player, but I think he's on too much money for us. I don't know if a deal is possible." Pericard, the hero of the Reading game, was unsure where his future lay with Juventus undecided if and when they needed him back in Italy and Pompey dithering about taking up a year's option. But Redknapp was sure of one thing: Pompey would be his last job in management. Just past his 56th birthday, Redknapp spoke as Glenn Roeder, the coach he brought to West Ham, battled in a hospital's intensive care unit to overcome a stress-related stroke. It might have been him or any of the other 90 or so managers who each week put themselves through an emotional wringer for three points and a step or two up a ladder. Redknapp had vowed when he left West Ham two years before to put an end to the anxiety and fear that seemingly pervaded every match and to start to live a normal life. But he missed it, the sweaty anticipation, the fantastic highs and even the deep, deep lows.

Sunday, April 27

PORTSMOUTH 3
ROTHERHAM UNITED 2

Leicester's lunchtime draw with Norwich left Pompey needing a win to clinch the title at the end of a long, extended battle with Micky Adams' side. It had been a two-team race from the end of August but now it was nearing its conclusion. Again, Fratton Park was packed out and again there was tension in the air. And again, just when it was most wanted, Pompey got a helping hand when Todorov fell under an innocuous challenge from Guy Branston. Merson made no mistake this time with his spot kick, his first goal at the Fratton End. But Branston got Pompey in a pickle when he latched on to Alan Lee's flick to score an equaliser. As ever, full of goals, Redknapp's side came back for Stone to set up Todorov to make

1-0 - Merson strikes from the penalty spot.

3-2 - Todorov scores his second and Pompey are champions.

CHAMPIONS

it 2-1, only for Chris Swailes to level again when he headed in a corner. But just before the break, Festa and Quashie combined for Pericard to head into the path of Todorov to score his second. Yakubu almost scored after coming on as a sub and Lee nearly equalised again with a header which flashed wide. Rotherham never gave up but Pompey held on and the celebrations started all over again.

Portsmouth (3-4-1-2): Hislop; Primus, Foxe, Festa; Stone, Sherwood, Quashie, Harper (De Zeeuw 45); Merson, Todorov, Pericard (Yakubu 68).
Subs (not used): Kawaguchi, O'Neil, Diabate.
Goals: Merson (11 pen), Todorov (22, 45).
Booked: Harper, Quashie.
Rotherham (4-4-2): Gray; S Barker, Swailes, McIntosh, Branston; Sedgwick (Monkhouse 80), Daws, Talbot (Warne 63), Hurst; R Barker, Lee.
Subs (not used): Pollitt, Hudson, Robins.
Goals: Branston (16), Swailes (29).
Booked: Sedgwick, Warne.
Attendance: 19,420.
Referee: R Beeby (Northamptonshire).

Promotion was having other repercussions with the reserves automatically elevated to the southern section of the Premier Reserve League, signing off from the Avon Combination with a four-goal thrashing of Swindon. Neil Barrett scored twice and Bradbury and Burton got the others. Paul Merson was also looking back and forward: "I can't believe, with all my addictions, that I'm lucky to be playing such a high class of football at 35. I'm not a killjoy or being negative but it's going to be much tougher next season. Where we have hammered teams week-in, week-out, we are now

The culmination of a wonderful season.

SLEEPING GIANT AWAKES

going to get hammered by the better teams. Going back to the Premiership is a bit special. It's a shame I won everything at Arsenal while I was still a kid. I did not appreciate it then because we won most of our matches. It will be a new challenge. You can have a poor start in the first division and catch up but you can't do that in the Premiership and expect to survive. In the first division you can look at ten games and expect to win them but you can't say that in the Premiership."

As supporters prepared to head to Bradford to round off a wonderful year, Mandaric and Peter Storrie were heading to Haifa to thrash out a permanent deal for Yakubu. The Nigerian had made it clear he wanted to play for Pompey and Maccabi backed down from their original demands of £4m. Mandaric, who had paid to borrow him, agreed a fee thought to be under £2m with 50 per cent of any profit heading the way of the Israeli club. The chairman was ecstatic about the deal: "He's a real jewel in the crown and I don't need to tell fans about his potential." As April ended, Pompey were already gearing up for life in a higher echelon. It was going to be exciting.

A sign of intent - Yakubu becomes a permanent Pompey player.

TOP 6 AT END OF APRIL 2003

	P	W	D	L	F	A	Pts
PORTSMOUTH	45	28	11	6	92	45	95
Leicester City	45	26	13	6	72	39	91
Sheffield United	45	23	11	11	72	50	80
Reading	45	25	4	16	61	45	79
Wolverhampton Wdrs	45	20	15	10	80	43	75
Nottingham Forest	45	20	13	12	80	48	73

13

GAMBLING ON SUCCESS

THE SEASON ENDED IN A blaze of glory at Bradford, but not before troubled Paul Merson had bared his soul in the 'Mail On Sunday' where he admitted that his gambling habit had returned with a vengeance. On the same day as the revelations appeared in print, Merson was playing his usual starring role in the 5-0 crushing of Bradford; football, as ever, providing the release from his private torments and demons. Merson said: "I have stayed away from drink and drugs but gambling has beat me, spanked me all over the place. Every day it would go through my head to commit suicide." Using the internet, telephone accounts and Teletext, Merson confessed to losing £30,000 betting on the outcome of a single football match.

Merson, who is married for a second time, told how he went to Florida on holidays with the children of his previous marriage and stayed rooted to his hotel room, gambling on American sports via a phone to his English bookmaker. Never once did he join the rest of his family at Disney World. He added: "I am a complete and utter compulsive gambler. I sat in a hotel room contemplating smashing my fingers just so I would not be able to pick up the telephone to ring my bookmaker. I have been on so many holidays with the kids in Florida and yet I have never been on a single ride at Disney World. How sad is that?"

During April, with Redknapp's permission, Merson spent a week at the famous clinic, 'Sporting Chance', under the watchful eye of its manager Peter Kay. Not that Pompey fans would have known or even guessed because Merson was still the consummate professional footballer, going about his business with style, grace, power and commitment, the qualities he had shown to such devastating effect throughout a long and eventful season.

Sunday, May 4

BRADFORD CITY 0
PORTSMOUTH 5

What a way to finish. Some 7,000 Pompey fans made the long journey to Yorkshire to pay

tribute to their team even though there was nothing riding on the match. Pompey's trips to Valley Parade had always been eventful in recent years. It was almost exactly five years previously that John Durnin scored twice and Sammy Igoe got the other as Pompey secured their first division status in a 3-1 win, Alan Ball reaching a peak of excitement as Manchester City were relegated instead. Plenty of flags and a gigantic snowstorm of ticker tape greeted the present-day Pompey players as they came on the pitch for the last time. But there was a reminder of less pleasant times. It was 18 years, again almost to the day, that fire ripped through an ancient wooden stand at Valley Parade, killing a number of trapped and terrified supporters. A minute's silence was properly observed.

And so to the action. Pompey showed why they were worthy champions with a devastating performance which ripped Bradford apart. For 30 minutes the match was evenly poised but once Gianluca Festa, the only outfield player not to have scored all season, put Pompey ahead

Todorov - finished off a remarkable season with a hat-trick at Bradford.

Left: Paul Merson - his confession to going off the rails with his gambling addiction shocked the football world. Luckily for Pompey, it had little effect on his on-field performances.

the rest of the match was a one-sided procession. Todorov, in a remarkable display of finishing, scored three including a penalty to end the season as the first division's leading scorer with 26 goals. Bookies at the start of the season were offering odds of 50-1 on him accomplishing that

**Steve Stone - added the
fifth in the rout
at Bradford.**

feat. Steve Stone added the fifth while Todorov's penalty was Pompey's 100th goal in all competitions. Bradford manager Nicky Law singled out Todorov as the difference between the sides, although that may have been unfair on the Bulgarian's colleagues, who were just as influential in yet another devastating away display. Law said: "Some of Portsmouth's one-touch football was unbelievable. People like Todorov and Merson are class acts while they are steady at the back. We lost our shape and discipline and you can't afford to do that against a quality team like Portsmouth. If we had Todorov up front it would have been a different game."

Redknapp could even afford to indulge in a little sentimentality in allowing patient Yoshikatsu Kawaguchi the chance to play as a second half substitute. Yoshi had sat on the bench for all the previous 48 games uncomplainingly so that some fans must have thought "subs (not used)" had become a prefix to his name. Yoshi did not disappoint, making up for lost time with a couple of blinding saves as Pompey completed a stunning victory, as so many away had been. In total they scored 101 goals in all competitions, failed to score in only three of the 49 matches and ended with 97 points. Redknapp said: "It was great for Festa to score in his last game for us. I only wish he could have stayed around. We scored 97 goals in the league and that's a remarkable achievement. I wish I had backed us at 33-1. I had a bet on Ipswich at 10-1, which shows what I know."

Merson, his addiction a Sunday talking-point across the nation, might not have appreciated that last comment. But Redknapp was sympathetic. His grandmother had been a bookie's runner and he and Jim Smith enjoyed a bet without it ever taking over and ruining their lives in the way it had with Merson. Redknapp said: "I know what he's going through. I probably understand gambling more than any manager because I like a bet. I know what it can do to people. Merse has had his problems with drink and drugs but he said to me gambling was the most evil because, when it goes against you, it does your brains in. He said the sad thing is that professional footballers only get one chance to earn big money. If you come out of it with nothing because you have gambled it all away that's very sad because you are never going to get the chance to earn that sort of money again."

Bradford (4-4-2): Davison; Uhlenbeek, Wetherall, Molenaar (Penford 53), Bower; Muirhead, Jorgensen, Francis, Myers; Gray, Forrest (Ten Heuvel 65).
Subs (not used): Wright, Magnusson, Sanasy.
Portsmouth (3-4-1-2): Hislop (Kawaguchi 45); Primus, Foxe (O'Neil 68), De Zeeuw; Stone, Sherwood, Quashie, Festa (Diabate 46); Merson; Yakubu, Todorov.
Subs (not used): Pericard, Burton.
Goals: Festa (20), Todorov (48, 50 pen, 58), Stone (67).
Attendance: 19,088.
Referee: S Baines (Derbyshire).

As Valley Parade, or the Bradford and Bingley Stadium as it was now known, emptied and joyous Pompey fans headed for their transport in a late spring afternoon, leaving a 'calling card' of a mountain of ticker-tape behind, thoughts turned back to the many triumphs of a season unique in Pompey's history. Unique because Pompey had never won a league so easily or with such a flourish or flair. They swept out of the first division with vigour, purpose and flamboyance in a torrent of goals, home and away. A team hastily put together over the summer months simply tore up the division week after week, month after month.

How did it happen? A number of factors came together so that everything fell into place in the right place, at the same time, a heady concoction of good fortune, good planning and failure by others. The crash of the ITV Digital contract took a heavy toll, not of clubs in the lower two divisions, as had been forecast by alleged experts who said 50 or 60 clubs would go out of business, but of those in the first division who had wage budgets way beyond their true earning capacities. Clubs in the second and third divisions survived the ITV Digital crisis because they had never relied on the money in the first place. But the effect on those in the first division and those dropping out of the Premiership was devastating. They froze. Unable to buy new players, they spent most of the 2002-03 season trying to offload their better, more expensive footballers simply to rid themselves of mounting, unsustainable debts. Pompey were the only team who spent the summer bringing in players, and they brought in quality at every turn. Leicester and Ipswich, both clubs held up as examples of what non-Metropolitan clubs could achieve in the Premiership, went into administration. Derby, who also came down, were in perpetual chaos, and teams like Wolves and Norwich, who had gone close to promotion the previous year, did not make many significant attempts to strengthen last summer.

While first division rivals, or those fancied to be rivals, came face to face with the reality of their poor financial management, Pompey filled up their squad with a never-ending supply of class players. "I never had anyone competing for the players I bought," was a Redknapp line, often repeated, and he was right. He brought in Merson, Stone and Sherwood, for instance, without so much as a hint of competition. Extraordinary. The total cost to Milan Mandaric was around £5m. Wages rose from £7m to £10m and there was another £4m spent on transfer fees, signing-on fees, agents' fees and other miscellaneous expenses, but this was offset to a degree by improved attendances and greater commercial activity. Promotion to the Premiership,

Tim Sherwood - a key signing by Redknapp who, along with Merson and Stone, provided the experience to the youthful exuberance and foreign flair at Fratton Park.

then, came at a small price compared with what champions of previous years had been obliged to pay to go up.

Redknapp's gambling instinct on footballers at least is based on a deep knowledge of players at all levels, their strengths, their weaknesses, and an equally deep love for the game. He likes players with pace, skill and flair and all those qualities came in abundance with the players he brought in during one of the biggest turnovers of all time in terms of players in and out of Fratton Park. Redknapp gambled on Merson having at least another year in him, gambled on Stone and Sherwood providing Premiership quality when they too had seen better days, and gambled on a host of others from the lower divisions, or from abroad in Yakubu's case. His biggest gamble was Todorov - and how he was vindicated. A failure at West Ham, Toddy did not show in his brief appearances in a Pompey shirt at the end of the previous season that he had anything special about him. But how opinions changed as he darted through first division defences with cunning, speed of foot and thought and fantastic finishing power. Redknapp's attack, attack policy surprised many opponents, which is why so many of the best results were achieved away, and Merson and Todorov were two prime examples of the Redknapp footballing philosophy.

It has to be said that the first division was not packed with quality, but that is not a reflection on Pompey's achievement or the way it was brought about. Mandaric supplied the money and gambled in his own way on Redknapp succeeding where others had failed him and left Redknapp to build not just a new team but a whole new club. Even his choice of Jim Smith as his number two was inspired. There are many challenges ahead. As Redknapp said, he was done a few favours during the championship-winning season by clubs in the Premiership, and those will cease. There is much to be done. The ground is inadequate, the training ground is poor and the team is not, overall, in the first flush of youth. But, for now, it is farewell to those perennial companions in relegation distress and hello to a bright new world.

Sheffield United could lay claim to being the outstanding team of the first division, reaching the play-offs and semi-finals in both cup competitions. Had they lost as quickly as Pompey did in the cups they might have contested the championship more consistently. But they did not. Leicester would have been worthy champions any other year, losing only six matches and finishing with a creditable 92 points. They had to survive the traumas of financial administration and the loss of one or two key players to balance the books. They had less flair than Pompey, scored fewer goals and were known as a team that were hard to beat. For them, the season 2002-03 was a wasted one and there was no sense of excitement or triumph once they too had secured promotion. But, overall, it was Pompey who proved over 46 games that they were conclusively the best side in the division. They played with imagination, excitement, daring and bravado, coming from the depths of the first division to claim a place among England's elite. Whatever happens in the future, the story of Portsmouth Football Club in 2002-03 will forever warm the hearts of fans wherever the game is played. It was a story of romantic charm, a story of enthusiasm rewarded. Above all, it was a story of triumph.

NATIONWIDE LEAGUE
DIVISION ONE
FINAL TABLE 2002-03

	P	W	D	L	F	A	Pts
PORTSMOUTH (C)	46	29	11	6	97	45	98
Leicester City (P)	46	26	14	6	73	40	92
Sheffield United	46	23	11	12	72	52	80
Reading	46	25	4	17	61	46	79
Wolverhampton Wdrs	46	20	16	10	81	44	76
Nottingham Forest	46	20	14	12	82	50	74
Ipswich Town	46	19	13	14	80	64	70
Norwich City	46	19	12	15	60	49	69
Millwall	46	19	9	18	59	69	66
Wimbledon	46	18	11	17	76	73	65
Gillingham	46	16	14	16	56	65	62
Preston North End	46	16	13	17	68	70	61
Watford	46	17	9	20	54	70	60
Crystal Palace	46	14	17	15	59	52	59
Rotherham United	46	15	14	17	62	62	59
Burnley	46	15	10	21	65	89	55
Walsall	46	15	9	22	57	69	54
Derby County	46	15	7	24	55	74	52
Bradford City	46	14	10	22	51	73	52
Coventry City	46	12	14	20	46	62	50
Stoke City	46	12	14	20	45	69	50
Sheffield Wed (R)	46	10	16	20	56	73	46
Brighton & HA (R)	46	11	12	23	49	67	45
Grimsby Town (R)	46	9	12	25	48	85	39

THE CAST

Producer
Milan Mandaric

Assistant Director
Jim Smith

Director
Harry Redknapp

Choreographer
Kevin Bond

Stage Hands
Andy Awford (coach)
Alan Knight MBE (goalkeeping coach)
Mark O'Connor (youth team manager)
Shaun North (youth team coach)
Gary Sadler (physio)
Dave Hurst (youth development officer)
Paul Hardyman (assistant youth development officer)
Stuart Morgan (chief scout)

Principle Players

Shaka Hislop (goalkeeper, born Hackney 22.2.69) Written off by West Ham following Redknapp's departure, Hislop was forced to flee the Premiership to rebuild his flagging reputation. But while the troubled Hammers endured a season-long battle against relegation, the Trinidadian provided a first-class foundation to Pompey's all-conquering side to prove his days in the top-flight are not yet numbered.

Arjan De Zeeuw (defender, Castricum 16.4.70) Former medical student De Zeeuw was just what the doctor ordered to restore Pompey's terminally-ill defence to good health. The Dutchman helped unfashionable Barnsley into the Premiership in 1998 and craved another shot at the big time after three years languishing in the second division with expensively assembled under-achievers Wigan.

Gianluca Festa (defender, Cagliari 15.3.69) 'Uncle Festa' lurched down to the south coast still reeling after being told he was no longer needed at Middlesbrough. The Italian's appearances were restricted by persistent knee problems but he still showed the qualities that helped him build up an enviable reputation in his homeland where he was one of the few players to shine for both AC and Inter Milan.

Hayden Foxe (defender, Sydney 23.6.77) Flame-haired Foxe ridiculed his teammates by arriving for training wearing his Australia kit following their 3-1 football friendly win over England just days after the Ashes debacle. The former West Ham star also poked fun at Glenn Roeder's claims he was not of Premiership quality with a string of outstanding displays in the heart of the Pompey defence.

Linvoy Primus (defender, Forest Gate 14.9.73) A devout Christian, Primus didn't seem to have a prayer of prolonging his Fratton Park career when Redknapp rebuilt the entire Blues defence in the summer. But the likeable Londoner managed to shrug off his unwanted association with the previous regime to establish himself as a regular in Pompey's new-look team.

Linvoy Primus

SLEEPING GIANT AWAKES

Matt Taylor (defender, Oxford 27.11.81) Highwayman Harry was accused of daylight robbery by Luton boss Joe Kinnear after snapping up Taylor for a reduced price of £750,000 but Pompey would raise five times that figure if the lightning-fast full-back was ever sold. Taylor's fantastic season propelled him into the England under-21 side and even drew comparisons with Brazilian World Cup winner Roberto Carlos among his appreciative teammates.

Kevin Harper (midfielder, Oldham 15.1.76) One of the surprise packages of the season, Harper looked to be on his way out of Fratton Park when Redknapp revealed his plans to reshape the team. But the former Derby player took full advantage of Stone's troublesome hamstring and left the manager with little choice but to offer him an extended contract with a series of impressive performances.

Paul Merson (midfielder, Northolt 20.3.68) Widely regarded as one of the most gifted players of modern times, Merson stunned the football world when he agreed to give up the grand surroundings of the Premiership for midweek trips to Grimsby and Rotherham. Critics believed the former England star was yearning for one final payday but the majestic midfielder proved his doubters wrong with a succession of awe-inspiring performances as Pompey's 'Captain Fantastic'.

Gary O'Neil (midfielder, Beckenham 18.5.83) As the only player plucked from Pompey's youth set-up to have appeared consistently in the first team, much was expected of O'Neil.

While the 20-year-old struggled to develop a stranglehold on the keenly contested midfield places, he proved an able deputy for Messrs Merson, Sherwood and Quashie to suggest he can handle the huge burden of expectation placed on his young shoulders.

Nigel Quashie (midfielder, Nunhead 20.7.78) Pompey supporters waited three seasons to see Quashie produce the kind of football that first persuaded Tony Pulis to bring him to Fratton Park back in the summer of 2000, but it was worth the wait. The former England under-21 star's new-found level of consistency made him an automatic first choice and prompted Merson to suggest the Blues had unearthed a future full international.

Nigel Quashie

SLEEPING GIANT AWAKES

Tim Sherwood (midfielder, St Albans 2.2.69) It was football's worst-kept secret but it still took Redknapp seven months to capture the signature he had coveted since before Pompey had even topped the table for the first time. Sherwood's well-documented feud with Spurs boss Glenn Hoddle meant the former England star had plenty of frustration to take out on the rest of the division and his arrival gave the promotion push a new lease of life.

Steve Stone (midfielder, Gateshead 20.8.71) Another Aston Villa refugee. Stone joined Pompey hoping to recreate the dazzling form that catapulted him into England's Euro 96 squad during his time at Forest. His long-term hamstring troubles stopped him making a consistent contribution to the team but, when fit, the balding winger still looked every inch a Premiership player.

Yakubu Ayegbeni (striker, Benin 22.11.82) With Pompey's promotion push threatening to lose momentum in mid-season, Redknapp went as far as Israel to sign 'The Yak' from Maccabi Haifa. It didn't take long for the Nigerian to show why he was rated at £4 million and the fans' fear of failure disappeared almost as soon as he stepped off the plane at Heathrow.

Svetoslav Todorov (striker, Dobrich 30.8.78) Signed by Redknapp for West Ham, Todorov was the first player to follow his mentor from east London to the south coast. After an unspectacular start, the sulky Bulgar of Upton Park became the Superstar Bulgarian of Fratton Park proving his £750,000 price tag was

money well spent as he became the most prolific Pompey striker since the days of 'Corporal Punishment'.

Vincent Pericard (striker, Efko, Cameroon 3.10.82) After failing at first to live up to the expectations of his Italian pedigree, Redknapp admitted he thought he had blundered by placing his faith in a player with no previous first team experience. But a run of five goals in as many matches showed the awkward Frenchman had more to his game than just an impressive set of dreadlocks as he proved the manager was wrong to doubt him.

Vincent Pericard

Understudies

Jason Crowe (defender, born Sidcup 30.9.78) After scoring just one goal in seven years as a professional, Crowe pushed himself forward as an unlikely attacking option with three goals in the space of four games to fight his way back into Redknapp's plans. Always performed well when called upon.

Eddie Howe (defender, Amersham 29.11.77) Ironically labelled 'Mr Reliable' by Redknapp on his arrival at Fratton Park from the manager's former club Bournemouth, Howe's miserable season lasted just nine minutes before he limped off with a campaign-ending knee injury on the opening day. The ex-England under-21 star spent a month in America undergoing surgery aimed at hastening his return to action at a time when his teammates were busy tying up their promotion.

Paul Ritchie (defender, Kirkcaldy 21.8.75) A member of Manchester City's first division championship-winning side in 2002, Ritchie was relegated to the reserves upon promotion to the Premiership. The Scotland international sustained a knee injury in only his third start in Pompey colours and played just one more game before being reunited with Kevin Keegan at the end of a solid but unspectacular three-month loan spell.

Efstathios Tavlaridis (defender, Serres 25.1.80) The Greek youngster was brought in to strengthen a defence depleted by injuries to Festa and De Zeeuw on the eve of the Manchester United cup tie, but he started only four games before being sent back to Highbury, picking up three yellow cards in the process.

Lassina Diabate (midfielder, Boigne 16.9.74) Few Pompey fans had ever heard of Diabate when Redknapp unveiled him as his ninth signing of the season in October but the Ivory Coast international left a lasting impression on opponents and teammates alike with his wholehearted approach. The former Auxerre ace picked up six bookings in his first 12 matches but his determination ensured he became a regular in the squad.

Lassina Diabate

Deon Burton (striker, Reading 25.10.77) After five seasons in the Premiership, Burton returned to the club which launched his career desperate to end his association with debt-ridden Derby. The Jamaican failed to recapture the form of his injury-interrupted loan spell after completing a permanent move back to the south coast, but he still showed glimpses of the form that took him to the World Cup in 1998.

The rest of the cast

Sasa Ilic (goalkeeper, born Melbourne 18.7.72) The Yugoslav had only been in English football a matter of months before becoming an overnight hero in Charlton's first division penalty shoot-out win over Sunderland in the 1998 play-off final. Ilic made seven appearances on loan at Pompey in September 2001 before re-signing from Hungarian side Zalaegerszeg on a short-term contract in February.

Yoshikatsu Kawaguchi (goalkeeper, Shizuoka 15.8.75) Adored by the fans but not favoured by the manager, Pompey's record signing starred alongside David Beckham and Roberto Carlos in a sportswear advert in the weeks leading up to the World Cup. But Yoshi spent the entire tournament watching from the bench after being dropped from Japan's starting eleven on the eve of the finals and the omission was followed by a season of reserve team football at Fratton Park.

Markus Heikkinen (defender, Helsinki 13.10.78) An international teammate of Southampton goalkeeper Antti Niemi, the Finn strolled into Pompey's Eastleigh training ground hoping to earn the chance to join his compatriot on the south coast. A substitute's appearance at Coventry was the highlight of Heikkinen's three-month trial but he proved a useful squad member during the closing weeks of the campaign.

Carl Tiler (defender, Sheffield 11.2.70) Part of the Charlton side that won the first division title in 2000, Tiler had few chances to win the hearts of the Fratton Park faithful. His own-goal winner against Norwich in December 2001 marked the beginning of the end for the centre back.

Jamie Vincent (defender, London 18.6.75) The only player signed by Claridge in his five months in charge, Vincent found himself reduced to a watching brief as his new teammates took the first division by storm. The left-back was brushed aside by the emergence of Taylor and remained an £800,000 outcast in the reserves.

Neil Barrett (midfielder, Tooting 24.12.81) Another of Rix's signings who did not find the new regime to his liking. A pre-season knee injury hampered Barrett's hopes of becoming a part of Redknapp's Fratton Park revolution and the former Chelsea star failed to make a single first-team appearance.

Shaun Cooper (midfielder, Isle of Wight 5.10.83) A product of Pompey's youth academy and held in high regard by Redknapp. While the manager ignored many more established first-teamers, Cooper was named in several squads early in the season.

Lee Bradbury (striker, Isle of Wight 3.7.75) A former squaddie who once patrolled the streets of Northern Ireland, Bradbury needed all the mental toughness he had built up in the forces to battle back from 12 months out with knee ligament damage. The former England under-21 international had two loan spells at Sheffield Wednesday before returning to Pompey for the final promotion push.

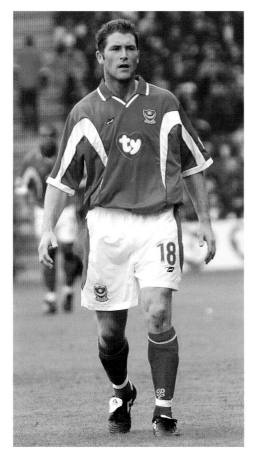

Lee Bradbury

Luke Nightingale (striker, Portsmouth 22.12.80) A failed loan spell at second division Swindon was all Nightingale had to show from another season of frustration. It was a far cry from five years ago when the striker marked his first-team debut with two goals against West Brom.

Courtney Pitt (midfielder, London 17.12.81) After coming through the ranks at Chelsea, the Londoner followed Rix to Fratton Park in the summer of 2001. Pitt scored two goals in Redknapp's first five games in charge but still found himself back on the fringes of the first team as he had been at Stamford Bridge.

Richard Hughes (midfielder, Glasgow 25.6.79) An Italian-raised Scot, Hughes possessed all the attributes needed to establish himself in Pompey's multi-national team. But the former Arsenal trainee lasted just seven games before suffering a recurrence of his long-term hamstring injury and Hughes spent the closing months of the season fighting to keep perennial strugglers Grimsby in Division One.

Carl Robinson (midfielder, Llandrindod Wells 13.10.76) The Welshman was given three months to prove his fitness after failing a medical in pre-season. But the former Wolves star found himself surplus to requirements and was sent out on loan to first Sheffield Wednesday then Walsall shortly after signing a three-year contract.

Mark Burchill (striker, Broxburn 18.8.80) Capped by Scotland as a teenager, Burchill scored four goals in his first five starts under Rix but joy turned to despair for Burchill when he damaged ligaments in his knee following a training ground collision with Robert Prosinecki. He failed to regain his first team place after 10 months on the sidelines and returned home to link up with Rix's assistant Jim Duffy at Dundee in January.

In the wings

Chris Tardif
(goalkeeper, 10.9.79)
Lewis Buxton
(defender, 10.12.83)
Carl Pettefer
(midfielder, 22.3.81)
Rowan Vine
(striker, 21.9.82)
Craig Bradshaw
(goalkeeper, born 31.7.84)
Lee Molyneaux
(defender, 16.1.83)
Terry Parker
(defender, 20.12.83)
Mark Casey
(midfielder, 9.10.82)
Anthony Pulis
(midfielder, 21.7.84)
Tom White
(midfielder, 30.10.81)
Chris Clark
(striker, 9.6.84)
Warren Hunt
(striker, 2.3.84)

Through the trap door

Dave Beasant
(goalkeeper, 20.3.59)
Justin Edinburgh
(defender, 18.12.69)
Ben Griffiths
(defender, 27.11.81)
Scott Hiley
(defender, 27.9.68)
Dave Waterman
(defender, 16.5.77)
Alessandro Zamperini
(defender, 15.8.82)
Garry Brady
(midfielder, 7.9.76)
Uliano Courville
(midfielder, 8.8.78)
Tom Curtis
(midfielder, 1.3.73)
Shaun Derry
(midfielder, 6.12.77)
Ceri Hughes
(midfielder, 26.2.71)
Stefani Miglioranzi
(midfielder, 20.9.77)
Michael Panopoulos
(midfielder, 9.10.76)
Robert Prosinecki
(midfielder, 12.1.69)
Mladen Rudonja
(midfielder, 26.7.71)
Thomas Thogersen
(midfielder, 2.4.68)
Rory Allen
(striker, 17.10.77)
Peter Crouch
(striker, 30.1.81)
Steve Lovell
(striker, 6.12.80)

SLEEPING GIANT AWAKES

PORTSMOUTH 2002-03 AT A GLANCE

Date	Venue	Opponents	Result	Pos	Scorers	Att
Aug 10	H	Nott'm Forest	2-0	7	Burton, Pericard	18,910
13	A	Sheff Utd	1-1	5	Burton	16,093
17	A	Crystal Palace	3-2	4	Crowe 2, Foxe	18,315
24	H	Watford	3-0	3	Todorov, Burton, Merson (p)	17,901
26	A	Grimsby	1-0	1	Burchill	5,770
31	H	Brighton	4-2	1	Taylor, Merson (p), Todorov, Crowe	19,031
Sep 7	A	Gillingham	3-1	1	Merson, Burchill, O'Neil	8,797
10	H	Peterborough	2-0	WC	Quashie, Primus	8,581
14	H	Millwall	1-0	1	Todorov	17,201
17	H	Wimbledon	4-1	1	Todorov, og, Taylor, Pericard	18,837
21	A	Norwich	0-1	1		21,335
28	H	Bradford	3-0	1	Quashie 2, Pericard	18,459
Oct 1	H	Wimbledon	1-3	WC	Pericard	11,754
5	A	Rotherham	3-2	1	Pericard, Todorov, Merson (p)	8,604
19	H	Coventry	1-1	1	Pericard	18,837
26	A	Burnley	3-0	1	Todorov, Harper, Quashie	15,788
29	H	Preston	3-2	1	Stone, Merson (p), Taylor	18,585
Nov 2	H	Leicester	0-2	1		19,107
6	A	Wolves	1-1	1	Merson	27,022
9	A	Derby	2-1	1	Todorov, Burchill	26,587
16	H	Stoke	3-0	1	Burchill, Todorov, Pericard	18,701
23	A	Sheff Wed	3-1	1	Todorov 2, O'Neil	16,602
30	H	Walsall	3-2	1	Quashie, Todorov, Taylor	17,701
Dec 7	A	Reading	0-0	1		23,462
14	A	Stoke	1-1	1	Crowe	13,330
21	H	Ipswich	1-1	1	Todorov	19,130
26	H	Crystal Palace	1-1	1	Merson	19,217
28	A	Nott'm Forest	2-1	1	Taylor, Pericard	28,165
Jan 1	A	Watford	2-2	1	Burton, Harper	15,048
4	A	Man Utd	4-1	FAC	Stone	67,222
11	H	Sheff Utd	1-2	1	O'Neil	18,882
18	A	Brighton	1-1	1	Todorov	6,848
Feb 1	H	Grimsby	3-0	1	Yakubu, og, Quashie	19,428
8	H	Derby	6-2	1	Yakubu 2, Todorov 2, Merson, Taylor	19,503
17	A	Leicester	1-1	1	Taylor	31,775
22	H	Gillingham	1-0	1	De Zeeuw	19,521
Mar 1	A	Millwall	5-0	1	Yakubu 2, Todorov, Merson (p), Sherwood	9,697
4	A	Wimbledon	1-2	1	Merson	10,356
12	H	Norwich	3-2	1	Todorov 2, Yakubu	19,221
15	H	Wolves	1-0	1	Stone	19,558
19	A	Coventry	4-0	1	Harper, og, Merson, Stone	13,922
22	A	Preston	1-1	1	Yakubu	16,665
Apr 5	A	Walsall	2-1	1	Harper, Todorov	7,899
12	H	Sheff Wed	1-2	2	Bradbury	19,524
15	H	Burnley	1-0	1	Todorov	19,221
18	A	Ipswich	0-3	2		29,396
21	H	Reading	3-0	1	Pericard 2, Todorov	19,535
27	H	Rotherham	3-2	1	Merson (p), Todorov 2	19,420
May 4	A	Bradford	5-0	1	Festa, Todorov 3, Stone	19,088

GOALSCORERS:

League (97): Todorov 26, Merson 12 (6 pens), Pericard 9, Yakubu 7, Taylor 7, Quashie 5, Burchill 4, Harper 4, Crowe 4, Burton 4, Stone 4, O'Neil 3, Foxe 1, Sherwood 1, De Zeeuw 1, Bradbury 1, Festa 1, OGs 3
Worthington Cup (3): Quashie 1, Primus 1, Pericard 1
FA Cup (1): Stone 1

PORTSMOUTH APPEARANCES AND GOALSCORERS
SEASON 2002/03

	APPEARANCES				GOALSCORERS			
	FL	WC	FAC	Total	FL	WC	FAC	Total
Lee Bradbury	3	0	0	3	1	0	0	1
Mark Burchill	4(14)	1(1)	0	5(15)	4	0	0	4
Deon Burton	11(4)	0	0(1)	11(5)	4	0	0	4
Lewis Buxton	0(1)	0	0	0(1)	0	0	0	0
Jason Crowe	7(9)	1	0	8(9)	4	0	0	4
Arjan De Zeeuw	35(3)	1	0	36(3)	1	0	0	1
Lassina Diabate	16(9)	0	1	17(9)	0	0	0	0
Gianluca Festa	27	2	0	29	1	0	0	1
Hayden Foxe	30(2)	0	1	31(2)	1	0	0	1
Kevin Harper	21(16)	1(1)	1	23(17)	4	0	0	4
Markus Heikkinen	0(2)	0	0	0(2)	0	0	0	0
Shaka Hislop	46	2	1	49	0	0	0	0
Eddie Howe	1	0	0	1	0	0	0	0
Richard Hughes	4(2)	1	0	5(2)	0	0	0	0
Yoshi Kawaguchi	0(1)	0	0	0(1)	0	0	0	0
Paul Merson	44(1)	2	1	47(1)	12	0	0	12
Gary O'Neil	11(20)	1	0(1)	12(21)	3	0	0	3
Vincent Pericard	18(14)	1(1)	0(1)	19(16)	9	1	0	10
Linvoy Primus	39(1)	2	1	42(1)	0	1	0	1
Nigel Quashie	42	1	1	44	5	1	0	6
Paul Ritchie	8(4)	1	0	9(4)	0	0	0	0
Carl Robinson	11(3)	1(1)	0	12(4)	0	0	0	0
Tim Sherwood	17	0	0	17	1	0	0	1
Steve Stone	18	0	1	19	4	0	1	5
Efstathios Tavlaridis	3(1)	0	1	4(1)	0	0	0	0
Matthew Taylor	35	2	1	38	7	0	0	7
Carl Tiler	0(2)	0	0	0(2)	0	0	0	0
Svetoslav Todorov	43(2)	2	1	46(2)	26	0	0	26
Yakubu Ayegbeni	12(2)	0	0	12(2)	7	0	0	7
Own Goals					3	0	0	3

KEY : ( ) = Appearances as substitute.
FL = Nationwide League, WC = Worthington Cup, FAC = FA Cup

DID YOU KNOW?

* Pompey's total of 98 points beat the previous club record of 91 points set by Bobby Campbell's Third Division championship side in 1982/83. It is also the second highest total for Nationwide League Division One since three points were awarded for a win; Sunderland hold the record with 105 points in 1998/99.

* The 29 league wins this season is another club record. The previous best was 27 in 1961/62 and 1982/83; on both occasions Pompey won the Third Division title.

* After only achieving ten away wins spread over the last four seasons, Pompey's total of 11 away victories equals the club record which was again set when they won the Third Division in 1961/62.

* Pompey's 97 league goals has beaten the previous record of 91 when they got promotion from the Fourth Division in 1979/80.

* Pompey's highest league attendance at Fratton Park this season was 19,558 against Wolverhampton Wanderers, which was the best since May 8 1993 when 24,955 saw Pompey beat Grimsby Town 2-1 in the final match of the season when they were pipped to the automatic promotion spot from Division One by West Ham United (coached by a certain Harry Redknapp) and subsequently lost in the play-offs to Leicester City.

* This is the third occasion that Pompey have won a championship title before the last game of the season. In 1948/49, they clinched the First Division at Bolton with three games to spare and in 1961/62 a victory over Watford decided the Third Division championship with two games left. This season, of course, Pompey won the title with one match in hand.

* Shaka Hislop's record of appearing in every match this season, including cup-ties, has made him the first Pompey player to achieve this feat since 1992/93 when Alan Knight, Alan McLoughlin and Guy Whittingham were all ever-presents. Knight holds the club record for a goalkeeper having been an ever-present on five occasions (1982/83, 1984/85, 1986/87, 1989/90 and 1992/93).

* Pompey's amazing sequence of scoring in 20 successive league games this season, from December 14 to April 15, was their best since the 1930/31 season when their run lasted 23 matches.

* No Division One team managed to complete a league double over Pompey during the season but they achieved it on nine occasions (Bradford City, Burnley, Derby County, Gillingham, Grimsby Town, Millwall, Nottingham Forest, Rotherham United and Walsall).

* Pompey has scored three goals or more on 20 occasions this season; 12 at home and 8 away.

* Pompey's team spirit this season is shown by the fact that, in ten league games, they have conceded a goal but have come back to either win or draw the match (5 wins, 5 draws).

* The contribution by Paul Merson and Matt Taylor to Pompey's success this season is best illustrated by the number of goals they have been involved in. Merson has had a 38.95% involvement; scoring 12 goals, providing the vital pass for 15 other goals while he initiated the move which led to a goal on ten other occasions. Taylor's contribution is 20.54% having scored seven goals, made 14 and started a move for five other goals.